HOME OFFICE

motorcycle

road craft

THE POLICE RIDERS' MANUAL

Her Majesty's Stationery Office London

ISBN 0 11 340149 3*

INTRODUCTION

This booklet, which succeeds former versions of Motor Cycle Roadcraft, has been prepared by police officers and embodies the knowledge and experience gained through years of riding under all conditions.

Accidents, with rare exceptions, do not occur at any given times and places, but rather in widely scattered areas and at all times of the day and night. Comparatively few of these incidents can be directly attributed to any particular road feature or vehicle defect, but it is found that in nine cases out of ten the cause of the accident can be traced to the failure of the 'human element' of the person or persons concerned.

The aim of the following chapters is to raise the reader's standard of riding to the highest possible degree of all-round efficiency. A motor cycle can be a lethal weapon and, like a gun, it should be handled with care; the advice which follows is not intended to reduce the pleasure to be gained from riding, in fact the opposite is true, the more confidence and knowledge at a rider's disposal, the greater is his capacity for enjoying and taking pride in his riding. Furthermore, if the reader follows this advice he may one day save somebody's life — perhaps his own.

CONTENTS

CONTENTS

CONTENTS

CHAPTER 1

THE SYSTEM OF MOTOR CYCLE CONTROL

Introduction

1 The prevention of road accidents has been a matter for public concern ever since vehicles first appeared. Accidents can occur at any time and place and cannot be attributed to any particular road feature or vehicle defect.

2 A common factor in accidents in which a vehicle is involved is the presence of a human being and the probability of human error. The human element is directly responsible for almost every accident and it is upon this aspect that attention must be focused. In addition to a high degree of skill, drivers and riders must show restraint and courtesy and the spirit of tolerance and consideration for others underlying the provisions of the Highway Code.

3 Many schemes and regulations have been introduced from time to time to try and reduce the number of accidents, but the most consistently successful has been the continued presence of the Police mobile patrols, who supervise the behaviour of other road users. Their own standard of riding must therefore be above reproach if they are to set a proper example and gain the respect and co-operation essential to their task.

4 The object of this manual is to raise the level of riding by teaching a uniform and methodical system which will provide an increased margin of safety at all times.

5 Riding includes starting the motor cycle, moving off, accelerating, steering it over different road surfaces, round bends and corners, in and out of premises, past other vehicles, progressing steadily through traffic, travelling at high speed if necessary, slowing down and eventually stopping. All this has to be done in complete safety, with no inconvenience to others and with minimum wear to the machine.

Rider and machine must blend harmoniously at all times. To assist in this respect, minor adjustments may be required to the controls so that they become extensions of the riders' hands and feet. The posture should be natural and comfortable, back very slightly bent, arms not quite straight to allow flexing at the elbows, with feet firmly placed on the footrests to provide a pivot for the body over uneven roads.

6 Quiet efficiency is the hallmark of the expert. Although alert he gives the impression of being completely relaxed. He rides in a calm, controlled style without fuss or flourish, progressing smoothly and unobtrusively. He will always be in the right place on the road, travelling at the right speed with the right gear engaged and he achieves this desirable state by concentrating all the time, planning ahead and riding systematically.

7 The rider of a motor cycle has a great deal to think about as continually changing conditions demand frequent alterations in course and speed. The surrounding traffic situation must be taken into account, including the proximity of other vehicles, the need to signal intentions, the surface conditions; in fact, a host of items to be thought about all the time.

8 The Police System of Motor Cycle Control creates a simple and repetitive method of riding which ensures that the rider omits no detail, leaves nothing to chance and when perfected gives that one ingredient essential to safe motor cycling — TIME TO REACT.

Definitions

9 THE SYSTEM OF MOTOR CYCLE CONTROL IS A SYSTEM OR DRILL, EACH FEATURE OF WHICH IS CONSIDERED, IN SEQUENCE, BY THE RIDER AT THE APPROACH TO ANY HAZARD. It is the basis upon which the whole technique of good motor cycling is built.

10 A hazard is anything which contains an element of actual or potential danger.

There are three main types:

(a) Physical features, such as a junction, roundabout, bend or hill crest;

(b) those created by the position or movement of other road users; and

(c) those created by variations in road surface or weather conditions.

11 By definition every feature of the System is considered at the approach to any hazard. Only those applicable to the particular circumstances are put into operation but whichever features are selected they must always be in the correct sequence. It is only by constant practice that skill in the application of the System can be acquired.

Features of the System

12 The FEATURES of the System of Motor Cycle Control are as follows:

(1) COURSE—The rider, having seen the hazard, decides on the correct line of approach. He looks in his mirrors and over his shoulder. If it is necessary to change position to obtain the correct course he considers a deviation signal.

(2) REAR OBSERVATION, SIGNALS AND SPEED—The view to the rear is again checked and, if the intention is to turn right or left at the hazard, consideration must be given to a deviation signal. Any reduction in speed for the hazard will be accomplished at this stage preceded by a slowing down signal if appropriate.

(3) GEAR—The correct gear is selected for the speed of the machine following application of the second feature, although intermediate gears may be passed through during the latter stage of any braking. The gears should not be selected to replace the brakes in their function of slowing the machine.

(4) REAR OBSERVATION AND SIGNALS—It is essential to take rear observation again and to consider a signal to deviate, if not previously given, or to emphasise an existing deviation signal.

(5) HORN—The horn is sounded if necessary.

(6) REAR OBSERVATION (LIFE SAVER)—A last look behind before deviating.

(7) ACCELERATION—The correct degree of acceleration is applied to leave the hazard safely.

Application of the System

13 For all hazards the seven features of the System of Motor Cycle Control must be considered but any change in conditions on the approach may require a complete re-assessment, starting again at Feature 1. For the purpose of the following examples it is assumed that the appropriate features can be applied without anything arising which might call for a change of plan.

RIGHT TURN

14 One of the most difficult and potentially dangerous manoeuvres is a right turn at cross roads because other road users may be entering the junction from any direction. The application of the System is illustrated in figure 1. As with all hazards the seven features of the System of Motor Cycle Control must be considered at the approach.

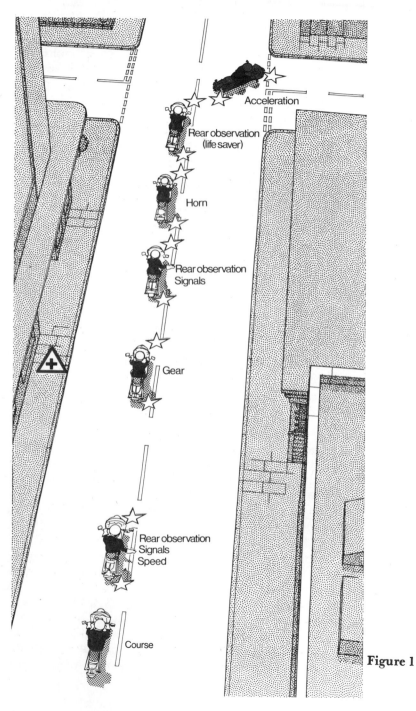

Acceleration

Rear observation
(life saver)

Horn

Rear observation
Signals

Gear

Rear observation
Signals
Speed

Course

Figure 1

Feature One—Course

15 The ideal course is just left of the centre of the road or into a lane designated for right turn traffic. If travelling in the nearside it will be necessary to move out and this should be done in plenty of time having regard to the volume of traffic and the speed of approach to the hazard. Advanced information can be obtained from direction or warning signs relating to the junction. A view to the rear is taken by looking in the mirrors and over the right shoulder. A deviation signal is given, if required, before moving out.

Feature Two—Rear Observation, Signals and Speed

16 With the motor cycle in the correct position on the road it will normally be necessary for the rider to reduce speed to that required to negotiate the turn safely. The view to the rear is again checked and the need for signals considered bearing in mind that the brakes may have to be applied and that other road users in front and behind should be informed of the intention to slow down and turn right. (The signal given at feature one may, of course, still be operating.) In the application of this feature the rider should aim to lose all unwanted road speed by braking, except for minor variations in speed when deceleration will be sufficient. If conditions on the approach to the hazard remain unchanged, no further braking should be necessary.

Feature Three—Gear

17 The gear selected should be appropriate to the road speed and one in which the machine will respond readily to throttle variations. Final adjustments to speed may be made in this way.

Feature Four—Rear Observation and Signals

18 Immediately after the gear change the rider should again use rear observation to check the movement and position of following traffic. He should consider whether to give a signal of his intention to deviate or whether an existing trafficator signal needs to be confirmed by arm.

Feature Five—Horn

19 No hard and fast rules can be laid down as to whether or not a horn warning should be sounded. The rider must be guided entirely by the circumstances, bearing in mind the need to make his presence known to other road users.

Feature Six—Rear Observation (Life Saver)

20 A last look over the right shoulder is essential to ensure that following traffic has reacted to the signals given and that it is safe to commence the turn.

Feature Seven—Acceleration

21 As he nears the junction the rider must consider the degree of acceleration required for the turn to be completed safely. Until the motor cycle has passed through the apex of the curve the speed as determined at feature two will be maintained, with the engine pulling but without an increase of road speed. This will ensure best possible stability and reduce the effects of forces acting on a motor cycle when turning. After the apex the rider may accelerate but the point at which this will occur must be related to the type of road surface and its condition. On a good dry surface acceleration may be applied just after the apex with a gradual increase as the path of the machine straightens out. If the road surface is poor acceleration may have to be delayed until the motor cycle is upright on a straight course.

LEFT TURN (See Figure 2)

Feature One—Course

22 The ideal course is well to the left of the road requiring little or no deviation from the rider's normal safety position. The view to the rear is checked and if circumstances require a change of position a deviation signal is considered before altering course.

Feature Two—Rear Observation, Signals and Speed

23 After rear observation, deviation and slowing down signals are considered before reducing speed. A turn to the left is normally slower than a right turn and the System will need to be started earlier.

Feature Three—Gear

24 The gear selected should be the most responsive for the speed at which the machine is being ridden.

Feature Four—Rear Observation and Signals

25 Immediately after the gear change the rider should again use rear observation and decide if a left turn signal is necessary or whether an arm signal is required to emphasise a trafficator signal previously given.

Acceleration

Rear observation
(life saver)

Horn

Rear observation
Signals

Gear

Rear observation
Signals
Speed

Course

Figure 2

Feature Five—Horn

26 Once again the rider must be guided by the circumstances (with particular consideration for pedestrians).

Feature Six—Rear Observation—(Lifesaver)

27 The final rear observation would be over the left shoulder.

Feature Seven—Acceleration

28 The rider must now consider the condition of the road surface in order to apply the correct degree of acceleration for the turn.

STRAIGHT AHEAD AT CROSS ROADS

Feature One—Course

29 The adoption of the correct course on the approach is of paramount importance as it will vary with the type of junction. The rider must take into account the need to obtain a clear view into the roads to the right and left, the position of other traffic, the presence of stationary vehicles, lane markings and all other circumstances before deciding on the best course. However, he must use the mirrors, look behind and before any change of position is made ensure that no danger or inconvenience is caused to others. A deviation signal would rarely be given as it would tend to confuse or mislead others as to his real intentions.

Feature Two—Rear Observation, Signals and Speed

30 With the machine in the right position the rider must assess, in relation to what he can see, the correct speed to negotiate the hazard. It cannot be stressed too strongly that the speed is related directly to the view available into the roads to the right and left. The more restricted the view the slower the speed. He should check behind and if it is necessary to reduce speed, consider a slowing down signal.

Feature Three—Gear

31 The correct gear must now be engaged for the road speed. This will enable the rider to accelerate out of the hazard if it is safe to do so, or stop more readily, if necessary.

Feature Four—Rear Observation and Signals

32 The position of following traffic should be noted but as the intention is to go straight on a deviation signal would not of course be required.

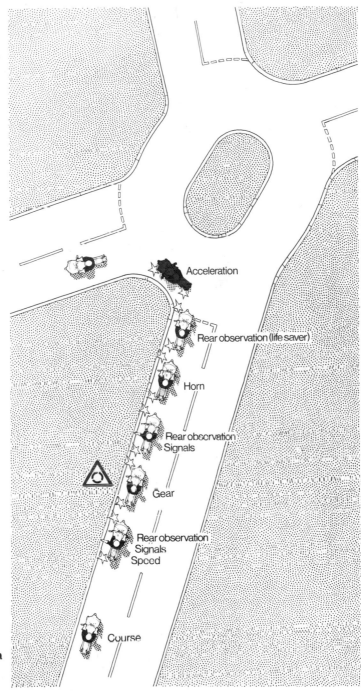

Acceleration

Rear observation (life saver)

Horn

Rear observation
Signals

Gear

Rear observation
Signals
Speed

Course

Figure 3a

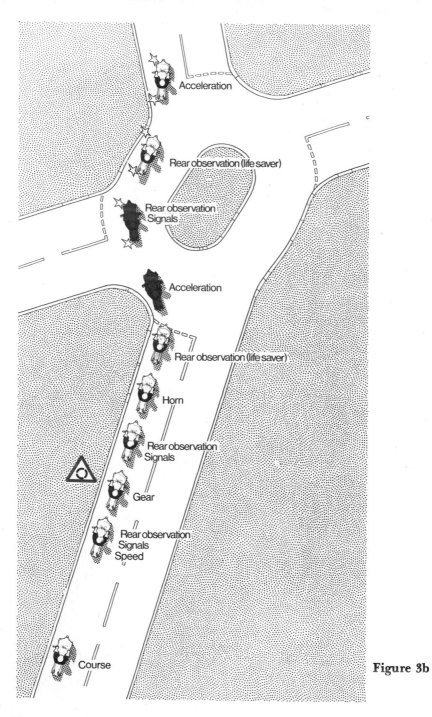

Figure 3b

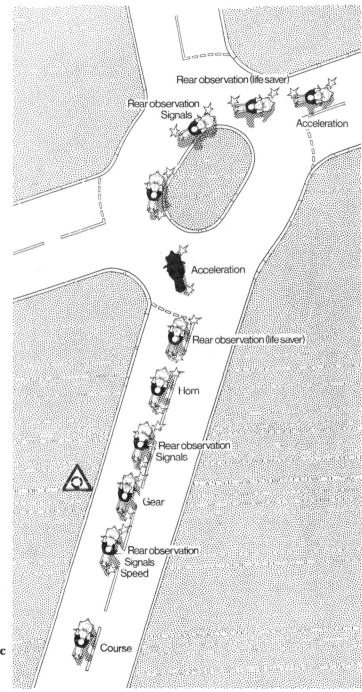

Figure 3c

Feature Five—Horn
33 The rider must assess the conditions and consider sounding the horn but it must not be used in the belief that it will ensure a safe passage.

Feature Six—Rear Observation (Lifesaver)
34 Not required as there is no deviation involved.

Feature Seven—Acceleration
35 Acceleration may be applied to leave the hazard once the rider is satisfied that he can safely continue.

ROUNDABOUTS

36 Roundabouts assist traffic flow at junctions by allowing traffic to enter and leave by different roads with the minimum of inconvenience or danger. They are one way systems in which traffic circulates in a clockwise direction and vary in size and shape from the 'mini' roundabout to the large gyratory complex. The System of Motor Cycle Control on the approach will be concerned with entering the roundabout. The general rule is to give way to traffic from the immediate right but to keep moving if the way is clear. Road markings may indicate otherwise.

Feature One—Course
37 The course selected will depend upon the intended direction of travel and the presence of other road users.

Where there is no other traffic following or in the vicinity and route directions permit, the best course is the shortest distance between the entrance and exit. Otherwise the course selected should be as follows:

(a) TURNING LEFT — Position on the approach should be in the nearside keeping to that position in the roundabout. (See figure 3a).

(b) STRAIGHT AHEAD — Position on the approach should be in the nearside unless conditions dictate otherwise. The chosen lane should be maintained through the roundabout. (See figure 3b.)

(c) TURNING RIGHT — Position on the approach should be to the offside keeping to that position in the roundabout. (See figure 3c.)
Rear observation is taken before the course is selected and any necessary signal given.

Feature Two—Rear Observation, Signals and Speed

38 It will normally be necessary to slow down for the roundabout having due regard to the need to give way to traffic from the immediate right. Traffic behind must be checked and a slow down signal given if required. If intending to turn left or right a deviation signal must also be considered.

Trafficator signals should be maintained through the roundabout.

Feature Three—Gear

39 The most responsive gear for the speed of the machine should now be selected.

Feature Four—Rear Observation and Signals

40 Immediately after the gear change the rider should check the situation behind. Directional signals should again be considered.

Feature Five—Horn

41 The use of the horn must now be considered.

Feature Six—Rear Observation (Lifesaver)

42 The look behind at the last moment before deviating.

Feature Seven—Acceleration

43 Before turning into the roundabout acceleration is considered but generally the contours of the roads and the close proximity of other hazards will render an increase of speed undesirable.

Negotiating the Roundabout

44 The hazards presented by the road layout and the movement of other vehicles must be dealt with as they arise by using the appropriate features of the System. A left deviation signal should be considered when opposite the junction before the one by which it is intended to leave. Acceleration to leave the roundabout should be applied as for a left turn not forgetting a final 'lifesaver' left.

CHILDREN PLAYING ON NEARSIDE FOOTPATH

Feature One—Course

45 The course selected should be one which gives the greatest possible margin of safety in relation to the children, i.e. a position further towards the crown of the road than the normal safety position, but having regard to oncoming traffic. The view to the rear must be checked and by early and gradual deviation the correct position adopted. A deviation signal would rarely be given because it may well mislead other road users, particularly following drivers who may interpret it incorrectly and attempt to overtake on the nearside.

Feature Two—Rear Observation, Signals and Speed

46 Rear observation will again be taken. Assessment of a safe speed for this hazard will depend on a number of factors, including how close it will be necessary to go to the children, the possibility that one or more of them may run into the road, the road surface, etc. A major reduction in speed by braking may possibly require a slowing down signal, but a deviation signal would not be given.

Feature Three—Gear

47 Whether or not speed has been reduced a lower gear may be required to give flexibility for that speed.

Feature Four—Rear Observation and Signals

48 Rear observation should again be used but no signals given.

Feature Five—Horn

49 The less the distance between the motor cycle and the children the more likely the need for a horn warning. This should be given early so they have time to react. Children are unpredictable and the giving of a horn warning does not guarantee the rider a safe passage through the hazard.

Feature Six—Rear Observation (Lifesaver)

50 Not required as there is no deviation to a new course.

Feature Seven—Acceleration

51 Once the rider is satisfied that he can continue normally he may accelerate away.

52 It will be seen from the examples given that the System of Motor Cycle Control is used on the approach to all hazards although every feature may not, in fact, be applied. Once the rider has learned the System he should practise it continually. He will find through experience that circumstances may alter on the approach to a hazard calling for a change of riding plan. The application of the System will become instinctive and form the basis upon which the finer points of riding can be built.

CHAPTER 2

ACCELERATION, GEAR CHANGING AND BRAKING

Acceleration

1 A thorough understanding of the System of Motor Cycle Control coupled with intelligent use of the throttle, gears and brakes is essential if the expertise associated with a skilled rider is to be developed.

2 'Acceleration' in this context means an increase of road speed of a motor cycle by opening the throttle. Conversely, speed may be reduced by closing it.

3 The acceleration capabilities of different machines vary considerably according to the efficiency of the engine and the power to weight ratio. An engine will respond to increased throttle openings only if it can develop the power to do the work demanded. All references to acceleration will assume that the correct gear is engaged and that the desired road speed is safe.

4 A good rider will use the throttle precisely, avoiding sudden and coarse movements which result in uneven acceleration. The carburettor is spring loaded to its closed position and the rider must accustom himself to the tension if he is to operate it smoothly. A defect or incorrect adjustment between the twist grip and the carburettor may defeat accurate control.

The Behaviour of a Motor Cycle under the Influence of Acceleration

5 Acceleration affects the behaviour of a motor cycle as it travels along the road. Figure 4 shows that, when under the influence of acceleration, a motor cycle tends to settle down on to the road at the rear improving the grip of the rear tyre on the road surface. This is a desirable condition when accelerating on the straight but care should be taken when riding through a curved path. The machine is most stable when the weight is evenly distributed, the engine just pulling with no increase in road speed.

Acceleration Sense

6 This is the ability of the rider to vary the speed of the machine by accurate use of the throttle control to meet changing road and traffic conditions. Acceleration sense can be

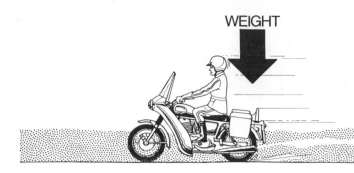

WEIGHT

Figure 4

applied to every facet of riding, e.g. following other vehicles, overtaking, approaching hazards and changes in road features. The essence is good observation coupled with sound judgement of speed and distance.

7 Lack of acceleration sense is often associated with applying acceleration to leave a hazard when it should have been obvious that braking would be demanded for a traffic hold-up ahead.

8 Similarly some riders maintain speed too long when coming up behind a slower moving vehicle and find it necessary to brake and wait momentarily before overtaking. A more skilled rider would have eased off a little earlier by using acceleration sense and approached and passed the vehicle at a constant speed.

9 The object of feature 7 in the System of Motor Cycle Control is to accelerate safely out of the hazard with due regard for the nature of the road surface.

10 The correct degree of acceleration in relation to the surface is important at all times but becomes more critical when the machine is ridden through a curved path. At the commencement of the curve the machine must be travelling at the correct speed which should remain constant until the apex has been passed. It must be appreciated that when a motor cycle is turning it will be necessary to increase power if the same speed is to be maintained. The point at which acceleration is commenced, and the amount applied, will depend on the state of the road surface. Should road conditions deteriorate it will be necessary to delay firm acceleration until the machine is upright.

By following this method of negotiating a curve the machine will always remain in a condition of maximum possible stability.

Acceleration can be delicate, normal or firm and the type used is very important, even on a straight road. The kind of road surface and the probable affect of the weather upon it must constantly be borne in mind. Firm or even normal acceleration may produce wheel spin on a wet cambered road or on a loose surface.

Gear Changing

11 Effective acceleration is possible only when a useful and economical increase in engine revolutions is obtained. The use of the gearbox must therefore be considered in conjunction with the capabilities of the machine.

12 One of the hallmarks of a good rider is the ability to change gear smoothly and make the best use of the gear ratios of the machine he is riding. The rider's judgment of the correct use of the gears available to him will improve if he has a good knowledge of the main components of the gearbox and their functions.

13 No matter how well a rider may handle a motor cycle his use of the gear box will do much to make or mar his riding. The essential ingredients are the ability to accurately match engine revolutions to road speed together with precise operation of clutch, throttle and gears. The first class rider should always aim:

(a) To be in the correct gear for every road speed and traffic situation.

(b) To make all gear changes quietly and smoothly.

(c) To know the approximate maximum road speed in each gear of the machine he is riding.

Moving from Stationary

14 If the controls are skilfully used, a motor cycle will be put into motion smoothly and its speed increased progressively by the use of higher gear ratios. Maximum acceleration through the gears will be necessary only on rare occasions of pressing need. Care must be taken not to 'over rev' in the lower gears nor to remain in a gear beyond the limits of its optimum performance.

Changing Down

15 When the speed of a motor cycle is reduced by a gradient, for traffic conditions or other hazards, a lower gear may be needed. A rider must develop his judgment of when to change to a lower gear.

16 A lower gear will be selected for one of two reasons; (a) loss of road speed to within the range of the next lower gear despite further opening of the throttle, and (b) on the approach to a hazard when a more responsive gear is required.

17 The selection of a suitable lower gear at the correct time will provide advantages in the following circumstances:

(a) On an up gradient, to maintain the power to climb the hill.

(b) On a steep down gradient, to control speed with engine compression, thereby avoiding long periods of hard braking.

(c) At the approach to a hazard, to enable the rider to accelerate out of the hazard, if this is safe, or to stop more readily if necessary.

(d) When travelling at low speeds or when in doubt about traffic conditions ahead, to provide the reserve of power and flexibility to accelerate or decelerate by control through the twist grip.

(e) On a slippery road, when the use of engine compression to lose speed is safer than braking, since the latter would be liable to cause skidding.

Faults

18 Common faults relating to the use of gears are:

(a) Poor co-ordination between foot and hand to effect a clean, smooth gear change.

(b) Inability to recognise by the sound of the engine when a gear change is required.

(c) Failure to select the correct gear for the existing road speed.

(d) Changing to a lower gear on a 'closing gap', e.g. inadequate braking followed by a gear change and hurried re-application of brakes.

(e) Changing down instead of braking (other than in the circumstances shown in paragraph 17e.

(f) Late gear changing, or entire failure to change down, at the approach to a hazard when the road speed and conditions demand a lower gear.

(g) Failure to match engine revolutions to road speed when changing down.

19 Machine sympathy is a quality to be developed in many ways not the least of which is gear changing. The rider who demonstrates delicacy and smoothness in his gear changing will be on the way to acquiring that polished style which is the ultimate aim.

Braking

20 More important than being able to accelerate and change gear is the ability to slow down or stop the machine when required. There are two ways in which this may be done.

(a) by deceleration, closing the throttle;

(b) by the application of the brakes.

The correct use of the brakes is a most important step towards safe riding. It must be understood what the results of braking will be if maximum efficiency is to be obtained.

21 When the throttle is closed the engine will slow down due to the compression in the cylinders and this slowing down will be transmitted to the rear wheel. Thus the engine is acting as a brake and the reduction of speed will be smooth and gradual with little wear to the machine.

22 The loss of road speed by engine deceleration will be more pronounced when a lower gear is engaged. This will be valuable when riding on slippery roads when normal braking could lock the wheels or where making long descents in hilly country but for normal riding requirements it is inefficient other than for minor variations in speed.

23 For normal riding a more efficient method of slowing down is to apply the brakes. Pressure on the brake controls can be varied at the discretion of the rider from a barely perceptible effect to such force that both wheels will lock. For all normal braking the initial free movement should be taken up gently and pressure progressively increased as necessary until it can be relaxed as the unwanted road speed is lost. When braking to a standstill the final effort should be so judged that the machine is brought to a gliding halt.

24 Apart from other considerations the speed of a motor cycle at any time must not exceed the speed at which it can be stopped within the distance the rider can see to be clear. The rider must know the distance he needs to slow down appreciably or stop from all road speeds. Not only must he know the distances he must be able to relate them to the road on which he is travelling. On a good dry road the average machine

should be capable of stopping in the following distances:

Speed in m.p.h.	Speed in ft/sec	Braking distance in feet
30	44	45
45	66	101
60	88	180
90	132	405

These distances will, of course, increase considerably in wet or slippery conditions. (A guide to the braking distance of a motor cycle in feet may be found by squaring the speed in m.p.h. and dividing by 20.)

25 To the braking distance must be added the distance travelled in the riders' reaction time to arrive at an overall stopping distance. Reaction time may be defined as the time that passes between the moment the rider observes the need for action and the moment he takes that action. The average rider takes 0.7 seconds from seeing an emergency situation to applying the brakes. The distance covered in that time is known as the 'thinking distance' and will be the same figure in feet as the speed in m.p.h., e.g. 30 m.p.h. = 30 feet. Thinking distance + braking distance = stopping distance.

26 The thinking distance will vary in three ways:

(a) with the speed of the machine.

(b) with the physical and mental condition of the rider.

(c) with the degree of concentration being applied.

27 Controlled, progressive braking is preferable to a sudden hard application. Figure 5 illustrates the behaviour of a moving motor cycle under the influence of braking. The weight is thrown forward and downward onto the front wheel and the rear tends to lift. The resulting unequal distribution of weight may reduce the general stability of the machine. This effect can be dangerous when banked over on a curved path.

28 To reduce these disadvantages as much as possible the following rules for braking should be applied:

(1) Brake firmly only when travelling in a straight line.

(2) Brake in plenty of time.

(3) Vary brake pressure according to the condition of the road surface.

(4) When descending a steep winding hill brake firmly on the

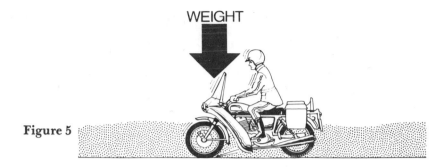

Figure 5

straight stretches and ease off in the bends. Remember the value of engaging a low gear at an early stage in the descent.

(5) Avoid using the front brake when the machine is banked over, turning, or on loose or hazardous road surfaces.

Braking under Normal Traffic Conditions

29 Loss of road speed on the approach to a hazard is Feature 2 of the System of Motor Cycle Control. Having observed the nature of the hazard and selected the appropriate course (Feature 1), the brakes will be applied as necessary to lose speed. When to apply the brakes and the pressures required will depend upon the initial speed, the road surface and the assessment of a safe speed for the hazard as it is approached. Braking may need to be firm but should never be fierce. The loss of speed should be constant and steady from the first movement of the brake controls to the point where the speed is right to enter the hazard; neither too early, so that it becomes necessary to accelerate towards the hazard, nor too late, so that a late and forceful application becomes necessary.

Influence of Braking on the Machine

30 Rule 1 of the rules for braking states that a rider should brake firmly only when travelling in a straight line. The importance of this rule cannot be too strongly stressed if maximum safety is to be ensured at all times.

31 Normally, when brakes are applied with the machine in an upright position, the weight tends to be thrown forward with the result that there is a very strong downward force operating on the front wheel. This increases the grip between tyre and road and, providing the braking system is in good condition, efficiency is improved.

32 With the forward movement of the weight the rear wheel tends to lift slightly in the initial stages of braking. That is why the rear wheel locks easily if the footbrake is applied too firmly. The result is that wheel and tyre bounce over the road and the braking effect is reduced.

33 With the machine banked over, as in negotiating a bend, braking becomes hazardous as the wheels may slide sideways. This is particularly true if the front brake is used.

Use and Distribution of Braking

34 On a good, dry surface, and for straight ahead braking, the distribution of total braking force required at each wheel to obtain minimum stopping distance is about 75 per cent front and 25 per cent rear. On a good but wet surface this is obtained with the distribution of about 50 per cent front and 50 per cent rear.

35 These figures can only be given as a general guide since much must depend on the circumstances. For braking at any speed on a good, dry road the front brake is the greatest asset. At the same time, all round braking efficiency is increased by a much lighter application of the rear brake, which will ensure that there is no tendency towards locking the rear wheel. On good but wet roads the front brake application is not so firm and a greater braking distance is required. At very low speeds, such as manoeuvring in heavy traffic situations, or bringing the machine to rest, the use of the rear brake only provides smoother control.

Use of Front Brake

36 Many untrained and inexperienced riders are quite wrongly apprehensive of using the front brake. They are unaware of its stopping capabilities when used with judgment and intelligence. Rule 5 of the rules of braking says 'Avoid' using the front brake on a slippery road rather than it must never be used. This is because, as more experience is gained, handling and general 'feel' of the machine under all combinations of road surface and weather conditions should be so perfected that it will be possible, if circumstances demand it, to use the front brake; but if it is used very delicate application will be called for.

Road Surfaces—Varying Brake Pressure

37 A surprising number of riders do not appreciate the value of good road surface observation. They ride on regardless and, in poor weather conditions when firm braking is called for, a collision or fall from the machine ensues, or at the very least the rider is badly shaken. By selecting that part of the road which will afford the best grip stability will be maintained and correct use of the brakes encouraged.

38 The main point to be borne in mind in connection with road surfaces is that brake pressure should vary with the road surfaces. A rough or dry surface should be selected for firm braking. Pressure should be eased off on a slippery patch. It must be remembered that loose gravel, dust and fallen leaves are almost as bad as grease or ice. A damp surface is more dangerous than a really wet one. A shower of rain after a long dry spell produces much more perilous surface conditions due to oil and rubber deposits.

39 When riding on treacherous surfaces it will generally be wise to dispense with the use of the brakes altogether and change to a lower gear and use engine retardation to slow the machine down. It will, of course, be necessary to use the rear brake to come to a final stop.

40 It is therefore extremely important to observe and react to the various types of road surface conditions from the moment the clutch is engaged at the start of the journey until the machine is finally brought safely to rest. The watchful rider will vary his accelerating, braking, positioning and general handling according to the type of road surface and prevailing weather conditions.

Emergency Braking—Good Dry Road
41 Brake design enables the rider to vary his effort on the brake controls to the extent that he can lock the road wheels. This is undesirable as the brakes are most effective when the wheels are still revolving just before they lock. In an emergency the rider must quickly assess at the time whether he has room in which to brake to a standstill on a straight course or steer out of trouble.

42 If he decides to brake the shortest stopping distance on a good dry road will be achieved by applying both brakes as hard as possible without locking the wheels. When the machine is banked over the rear brake only should be used and not until the machine is in the upright position should the front brake be firmly applied. If it comes to the point where it is either a case of braking hard or colliding with another vehicle or object it is most certainly better to apply the rear brake hard and at the same time lay the machine yet farther over. If the front brake is used other than lightly with the machine banked over the front wheel will tend to slide outwards in the opposite direction with the result that the tyre will lose its grip on the road.

Emergency Braking—Slippery Road
43 Wet, adverse cambered surfaces or where the surface is loose, greasy, icy, highly polished or covered with leaves present a severe problem. In an emergency the advice given in paragraph 34 should be followed and braking effort evenly divided between front and rear when the machine is upright. When banked over the use of the front brake is extremely hazardous and it should be applied with great caution only as a last resort.

Brake Test
44 The correct operation of the brakes is vital to proper control of a machine. A rider should check the operation of the hand and foot controls before riding the machine and as soon as possible after moving off test both brakes under running conditions. This test should ideally be carried out at a speed of 30 m.p.h. in top gear on a level stretch of road with a good surface but it may be necessary to compromise in some respects. The object of the test is to see how the machine responds to a normal application of the brakes when applied firmly and progressively. The machine should pull up on a straight course with the clutch engaged until it is necessary to disengage it to prevent the engine from stalling.

DUE REGARD MUST BE GIVEN TO THE SAFETY AND CONVENIENCE OF OTHER ROAD USERS.

CHAPTER 3

RIDERS' SIGNALS

1 Signals are the means by which riders warn other road users of their intentions and presence. They are the language of the road. If they are to be understood they must be as illustrated in the Highway Code. To be of any use they must be given clearly and in good time.

2 Signals are informative in that they may give notice of an intention to carry out a manoeuvre. They give a warning not an instruction and give no right whatsoever to carry out the intended action unless it is safe.

3 Riders' signals are divided for the purpose of this chapter into the categories shown below:

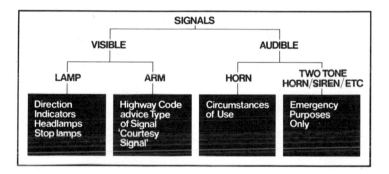

VISIBLE SIGNALS

Lamp
5 The meanings of the direction indicator signals illustrated in the Highway Code are as follows:

(a) I intend to move out to the right or turn right.

(b) I intend to move in to the left or turn left or stop on the left.

6 Care should be taken when the left indicator is used as a signal for stopping on the nearside just past a junction on the left. This could be misleading as, for example, a driver waiting in the road on the left may move out, thinking that the approaching machine is going to turn left.

7 A common fault is that of leaving the indicator in operation long after the turn has been completed. It follows that a rider waiting to emerge from a side turning should not accept an indicator signal as complete proof of another road user's intention. He should wait for supporting evidence, e.g. a considerable reduction in speed, before moving out.

8 Another form of signalling by lamp is that of flashing the headlight during the hours of darkness. This is an effective means of giving warning of approach to a road junction or to a driver before overtaking him. The headlight should be used in good time for junctions but other road users must not be dazzled. (See also Chapter 4 paras 38 to 44.)

9 The flashing of the headlight should not be used for signalling in daylight unless in lieu of a horn warning for overtaking at speed on motorways, dual carriageways, and other fast roads when the System and, therefore, the warning of approach will be earlier than on other types of roads. The length of the warning will be determined by the circumstances existing at the time but in any case should consist of only one flash. The use of this form of signalling calls for care as it is becoming the practice for many drivers to interpret a headlamp flash as an invitation to take precedence.

10 The stop lamp fitted to the rear of the machine and operating with the brake controls is a useful form of signal. In circumstances where advance warning should be given of the intention to slow down or stop, e.g. at a pedestrian crossing, the arm signal should be used.

Arm

11 The Highway Code illustrates the arm signals to be given when indicators or stop lights are faulty, or to emphasise and confirm previously given signals.

(a) 'I INTEND TO MOVE OUT TO THE RIGHT OR TURN RIGHT'. The palm of the hand faces the front, fingers extended and close together, the forearm held parallel to the ground.

(b) 'I INTEND TO MOVE IN TO THE LEFT OR TURN LEFT'. This signal is given as at (a) above, but with the left arm.

(c) 'I INTEND TO SLOW DOWN OR STOP'. The right arm is used as in (a) above, but with the palm of the hand facing the ground. The arm is slowly lowered and raised two or three times.

12 The expert rider will not only give exemplary signals himself but will also know the signals given by other road users. Signals to go ahead given by unauthorised persons must not be relied upon but a signal to stop given by anybody should be treated with due respect in the interests of safety. There may have been an accident, etc.

13 It is appropriate here to include a mention of the courtesy signal, i.e. an acknowledgement of a courtesy extended by another road user by raising the hand. It should not be overdone nor should it be neglected for its general use can do much to promote good road manners.

14 Visible signals should always be linked with rear observation. 'Rear observation' before 'Signals' will become a habit and ensure that necessary signals are given to following traffic.

AUDIBLE SIGNALS

Horn

15 The horn should be sounded only when it is really necessary. No hard and fast rules can be laid down but there are certain occasions when the use of the horn is justified even though every other precaution has been taken.

- (a) To attract the attention of another road user who is obviously vulnerable. Pedestrians and cyclists, particularly children, are usually involved.

- (b) When approaching a hazard where the view is very limited, such as a blind bend.

- (c) Prior to overtaking, bearing in mind the following:

    - (i) Is the driver in front aware he is about to be overtaken.

    - (ii) Can he be given plenty of room in case he should deviate slightly.

    - (iii) Will unexpected overtaking at speed be likely to disturb him.

16 Experience, intuition and the possibility of adopting an alternative riding plan must be the criteria upon which a rider decides to sound, or not to sound, the horn. In heavy traffic occasions for using the horn are rare, primarily because speeds are moderate and other action can be taken in good time.

17 The horn warning should be confined as far as possible to one note, either short or long, according to traffic conditions

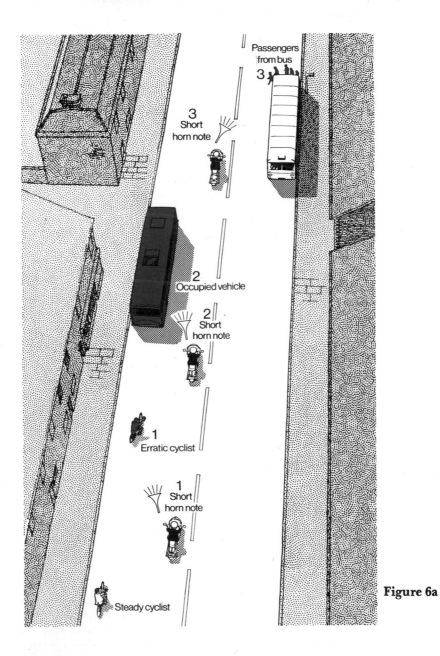

Passengers
from bus
3

3
Short
horn note

2
Occupied vehicle

2
Short
horn note

1
Erratic cyclist

1
Short
horn note

Steady cyclist

Figure 6a

and the type of road user for whom it is sounded. Figures 6a
and b show some common occasions for the use of the short or
long note.

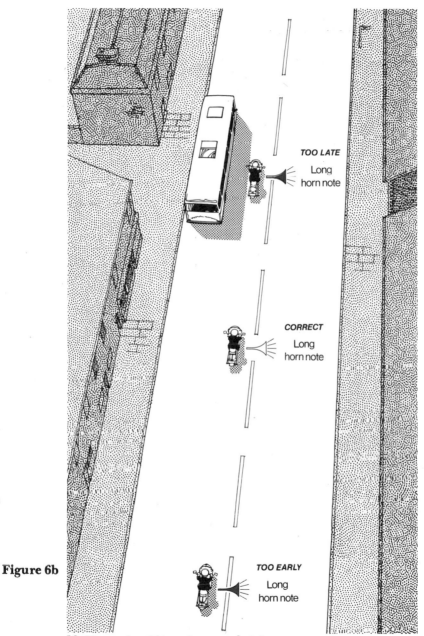

Figure 6b

18 Horns should not be sounded in an aggressive or demanding manner, but always courteously, giving plenty of time for other road users to react.

Two Tone Horns/Sirens, etc.

19 Two tone horns, sirens etc., are fitted to police vehicles for use when a police driver or rider engaged upon an urgent assignment is being impeded and he needs to obtain a clear passage through traffic. Most drivers on hearing the warning of an approaching emergency service vehicle will endeavour to allow precedence to it but the police rider must understand that the use of the warning instrument gives him NO PROTECTION OR RIGHT OF WAY WHATSOEVER. He must never ride at a speed faster than is safe for the conditions nor other than in accordance with the instructions in this manual. His duty to the public generally, and himself is quite clear in this respect.

CHAPTER 4

OBSERVATION

1 The object of this chapter is to assist the rider to improve his standard of road observation by considering individual aspects of the subject.

Concentration
2 Good vision, hearing and standard of health, all have a bearing on the amount of concentration which can be given to any activity at any one time.

3 The ability to concentrate exists in everyone, but few can concentrate sufficiently to ride a motor cycle with complete mastery for very long. The rider must therefore adjust the speed of his machine to the degree of concentration he is able to apply at the time. Without self discipline attention is inclined to wander from essential points of observation. A conscious effort must be made to prevent this.

Concentration and Road Observation
4 These are very closely related, for without the former success in the latter cannot possibly be achieved. It is not enough merely to see every detail in a road scene; the value of what is seen must be assessed and upon that value a riding plan formulated. Even though a rider may be expert in handling the machine, the standard of safety and consideration for other road users will not be satisfactory until the habit of good observation is cultivated.

5 The rider must aim to maintain the best possible view at all times. This can only be achieved by ensuring his windshield is kept clean inside and outside and that he is wearing a suitable visor, or goggles, to protect his eyes. He should ensure his mirrors are clean and properly adjusted.

Riding Plans
6 Riding plans should be made on the correct assessment of the ever changing scene ahead and to the rear of the motor cycle. The rider should be able to make decisions without hesitation in a methodical manner at any moment. All decisions must be based on the principle of safety for others as well as for himself.

7 Riding plans and decisions are made on a combination of:

(a) What can be seen.

(b) What cannot be seen.

(c) The circumstances which may reasonably be expected to develop.

Decisions can rarely be based solely on (a) because there are many stretches of road where the layout and traffic conditions do not permit the rider an unobstructed view. The greatest difficulties arise from areas into which the rider cannot see, such as around bends and corners, behind trees and buildings, at places where roads converge or where other traffic obstructs the view of the road beyond. In these circumstances in particular the rider must be able to stop his machine in the distance he can see to be clear.

8 Allowances should always be made for the mistakes of other road users. The rider of a motor cycle should never fail to appreciate the vulnerability of certain classes of road users, the aged, the infirm, the blind and young children. It is unsafe to assume that another driver will react correctly to any given situation; he may have passed his test only that day or be driving a strange or defective vehicle. He may be naturally aggressive or thoughtless, or attempting to drive beyond his capabilities to keep an urgent appointment. Riding to the System will prevent a rider from becoming involved in an accident for which he is directly responsible. By concentration, early recognition of potential danger and a defensive attitude of mind he will also avoid accidents which could result from the mistakes of others.

9 Riding plans, therefore, must be based on what is actually observed, the assumption that there may be danger in every obscured section of road and that others may do something foolish at any moment.

How Vision is Affected by Speed

10 Crowds of pedestrians can move about on the pavements without colliding with one another, not so much because they are looking out for obstructions, but mainly because their speed of movement is so slow that they can change their pace and direction in time to avoid a collision. If, however, one of them wishes to get along quickly he has to look further ahead, and vary his course and speed accordingly. He then finds that his view of other pedestrians at close quarters deteriorates, so that quite often if one of them comes into his path suddenly they may collide.

11 The rider of a motor cycle, adjusts the length and breadth of his vision in a similar way, but of course, over greater distances. As speed increases so his focal point must be moved further ahead for objects there to appear clear and well defined. Objects in the foreground become less distinct.

12 When road speed must be kept low because of traffic conditions, the focal point needs to be closer for the rider to observe foreground details. These often indicate that a dangerous situation is developing and he then has time, owing to his low speed, to take precautions which will prevent him from becoming involved.

13 The rider must therefore focus his eyes according to speed and when there are many foreground details to be seen speed must be kept low if collisions are to be avoided. It is clearly dangerous to ride fast in the wrong places.

14 Continuous riding for long periods may result in fatigue which will cause eye strain and lack of concentration. Although special efforts may be made by the rider to maintain his normal standard of observation he will find that the task becomes increasingly difficult. His recognition and assessments of dangerous situations will become late and inaccurate.

Weather Conditions
15 Weather conditions such as fog, mist, heavy rain or snow, the fading daylight and bright sunshine reduce visibility considerably. To meet these conditions speed must be reduced so that objects in the immediate foreground may be seen in time to take any necessary action.

16 In daylight fog or conditions of poor visibility, the headlamp must be switched on. A clearer view may be obtained by cleaning the visor or goggles, or by removing them completely, A slow steady pace should be maintained using the edge of the carriageway, hazard lines and reflective studs (cats eyes) as a guide especially when approaching a road junction or corner. Be prepared for sudden stoppages of traffic ahead and do not follow too closely. Traffic should be overtaken only when it is absolutely safe and will seldom be possible in fog on a two way road.

Road Surfaces
17 The average rider is not so well acquainted with the road surface types and conditions as he should be. It is useless to

complain about a slippery surface after a fall. A good rider is the one who looks well ahead, recognises any change in road surfaces conditions and then applies correct values of braking, acceleration and steering so that maximum road holding is always achieved.

18 When clean and dry the surfaces of most properly made up roads are good or fairly good for road holding. In wet weather they may become slippery particularly during a shower of rain following a long spell of dry weather. The presence of snow, frost, ice, oil, moist muddy patches or wet leaves, dry loose dust or gravel etc., can cause tyres to lose adhesion.

19 The adverse surfaces mentioned in para. 18 are all recognisable and they have their own distinctive appearances. Unfortunately, these conditions are frequently found at the approach to, or at, hazards where steering, braking and acceleration may need alteration and tyre adhesion is then of paramount importance. A common hazard today is the deposit of diesel fuel on the road usually at roundabouts, corners and bends. It is normally visible on dry surfaces, invisible on wet surfaces but can sometimes be detected by its distinctive odour.

20 Most roads have a surface of asphalt or other compounds which may have a dressing of stones or chips. These have a comparatively high non-skid value and are easily recognised. In time they take on a polished appearance and lose some of their non-skid properties.

21 Concrete road surfaces usually have a distinctive appearance, through being light in colour, some have a roughened formation of lateral ribs, most have a good non-skid value. Some, however, are apt to hold surface water which in cold weather freezes, creating a slippery surface which is not easily seen.

22 Wood blocks and stone setts are encountered occasionally in towns and cities. Great care must be taken when riding on these surfaces to avoid skidding, which will occur from the slightest cause, especially when wet.

23 During wintry weather, road surfaces become frost and ice covered, but not always uniformly. Isolated patches and certain gradients remain iced up when other parts have thawed out. The good rider should be on the look out for these areas and recognise them not only from their appearance but from the behaviour of other vehicles, and will take due precautions in good time to avoid skidding. Remember, tyres travelling on ice make virtually no noise.

24 To maintain stability a good look out must be kept for pot-holes, projecting man hole covers, sunken gullies and metal or painted carriageway markings. To avoid these the course must be altered slightly if this can be done without inconvenience to other road users. If they cannot be avoided, speed must be reduced.

Road Signs and Markings

25 There are many road signs and markings and it is important for the information or directions they give to be understood. Every sign or road marking must be seen in good time if the rider is to comply with it or profit from the information given.

26 Having seen the sign and understood its meaning, the rider should look beyond it to the road layout or condition to which it refers. He will then have ample opportunity to assess the situation and formulate a safe riding plan.

27 It is disturbing but true that the average road user does not see and understand the majority of the signs provided for his guidance, unless he makes a conscious effort or is in search of specific information. Every rider should cultivate a special interest in and respect for all signs and markings; by doing so he will improve his road observation and general standard of road behaviour.

Zones of Visibility

28 The area ahead of the rider is divided into zones where his view is good and zones where his view is obstructed. It is essential when approaching areas of potential danger where view is restricted to make maximum use of all available aids so that riding may be planned accordingly.

29 Figure 7 illustrates a crossroads and the improving view available to the rider on his approach as he applies the features of the System. From V1 to V3 the view improves very little, which shows how necessary it is to approach the hazard with special care. From V4 the view into the converging roads rapidly improves enabling the rider to make his decision to maintain or increase speed, slow down or stop, according to the position and behaviour of other road users.

30 The observant rider will take full advantage of open spaces and breaks in hedges, fences or walls, to get that valuable if brief, view into converging roads which to some riders appear totally obscured. It is often possible to judge the severity of any

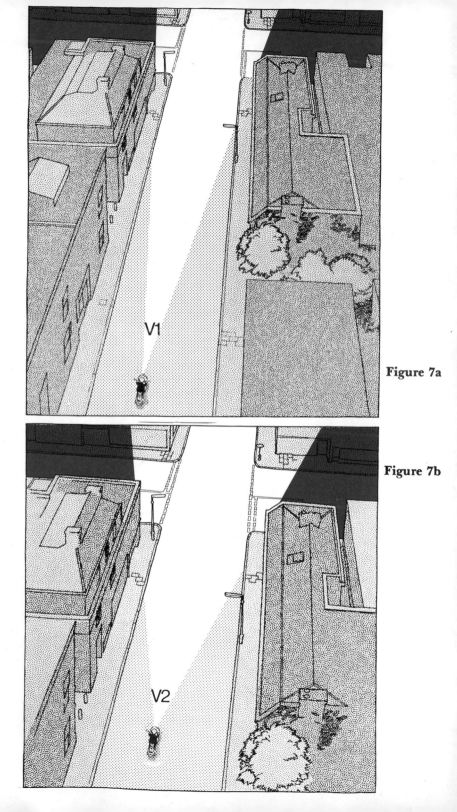

Figure 7a

Figure 7b

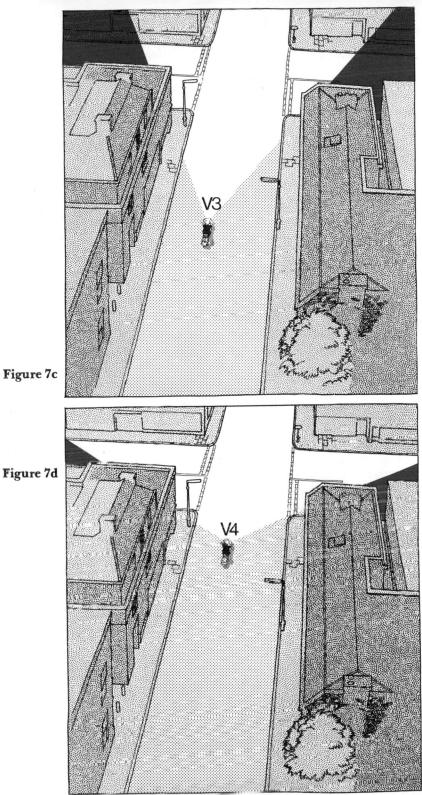

Figure 7c

Figure 7d

bend or gradient by the position, etc., of trees, hedges and other features. Figures 8a and b illustrate the zones at the approach to a crossroad where the view is restricted. The zone on the rider's right is broken up by gaps in the wall which runs alongside the road. View into the nearside converging road is at first quite poor, but the set back of the hedge at the actual junction provides a superior view at a later stage to that on the offside, which becomes poor again owing to the presence of the wall.

31 The rider should also be aware of the limited view in relation to stationary and moving vehicles ahead which can be improved to some extent by early appreciation and correct positioning. This subject will be discussed more fully in Chapter 5. The main point to remember is that the closer the vehicle is to the one ahead the less the rider can see.

Aids to Good Road Observation

32 One of the most important aids to successful riding is local knowledge. To know the situation of main road junctions, one-way streets and roundabout systems is undoubtedly of great assistance to the rider but his riding plan for each hazard must be based on the prevailing conditions, rather than what is normally found there.

33 Town riding in particular demands complete concentration, road observation, the ability to react quickly to changing situations and considerable riding skill. Views ahead are frequently restricted owing to the density of the traffic. It is not wise to focus all ones attention on the vehicle immediately in front and a sensible distance should be maintained behind it so that a view of traffic movement two or three vehicles ahead is obtained from time to time.

34 In places where traffic is really heavy and slow, riding is nothing more than a series of stops and starts. Length of view is short and passage along the road becomes a matter of 'following my leader'. If, however, there are two or three lines of traffic moving in the same direction it is important to be in the correct lane especially if a turn to the left or right is to be made at the next junction.

35 An accurate forecast of traffic movement can sometimes be made by observing quite small details. It is frequently possible to notice something and to link what is seen with the possibility of something else happening. An obvious example of this is when following a bus. The rider should be aware of the possi-

bility of it stopping further along the road particularly if passengers are seen moving towards the exit. A complete list cannot be given but the following further examples will be of use:

OBSERVATION LINKS

Traffic is turning ahead.	Other vehicles may emerge.
Pedestrian hails cab.	Cab may stop suddenly, or turn, or move away from rank. Pedestrian may step into road.
A row of parked vehicles.	Doors may open, vehicles may move off. Pedestrians may step out from between vehicles. Small children may be hidden from view.
Ice cream vans, mobile shops, school buses, etc.	Pedestrians, particularly children, are likely to be in the vicinity.
Bus at stopping place.	Pedestrians crossing road to board or after alighting. Bus moving off possibly at an angle.
Pedal cyclist.	Glancing over shoulder, may then turn right. Strong wind may cause wobble.
Fresh mud or other deposits on road. Newly mown grass, etc.	Slow moving vehicles or animals just around a bend.
Post Office vans, tradesmen's vehicles, etc.	May stop at associated premises, e.g. Post Office, shops, public houses, garages, building sites, etc.
Pull in's, petrol stations, public houses, parking places, etc.	Movement of vehicles in and out.
Motorway access points.	Vehicles in nearside lane may move out.
Green traffic lights.	May change.

No matter how good a rider's observation may be it can only be of assistance to him if he forms a correct assessment of what he sees and takes the appropriate action or precautions. It is not enough to react merely to what is seen. A positive effort must be made to look for the clues from which an accurate

Figure 8a

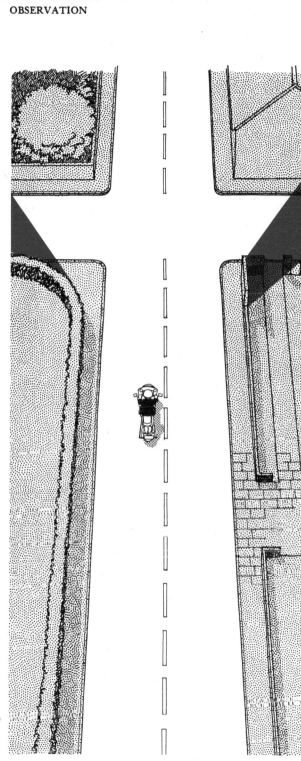

Figure 8b

prediction can be made, e.g. shadows on road, reflections in shop windows, exhaust smoke from stationary vehicles, and so on.

Rear Observation

36 Much has been said about forward observation but it must not be overlooked that it is equally and, in certain circumstances, even more important that the rider should be aware of the conditions behind him. It is of no value to look back or check the rear view mirror without really observing what is behind, or to take two or more rear observations when one would suffice. Looking to the rear when following closely behind another vehicle, without allowing for the possibility that it may suddenly stop, is just as foolish as failing to look back before actually overtaking. Prior to a hazard, the view obtained in the mirror should be confirmed by looking to the rear.

37 Rear observation should be made at the appropriate points shown in the System of Motor Cycle Control. However, the System is sufficiently flexible to permit further rear observation if traffic conditions or other circumstances make it necessary.

Night Riding

38 Whilst this section is headed 'Night Riding' it should be borne in mind that the expression 'Night' in this context applies to the period from the end of the day when light begins to fail until full light the following day. During this time lights must be switched on.

39 In built up areas where visibility is poor a dipped headlamp should be used so that the riders view is extended and other road users can see his machine more easily. On unlit roads the headlamp should be on main beam unless dipped beam is required because of opposing traffic or when following other vehicles. However, there are occasions when a dipped headlamp instead of main beam can be used to advantage to illuminate areas which may not otherwise be seen (e.g. when negotiating left hand bends or at hump back bridges).

40 All lamps must be kept clean and the headlamp correctly set so as to provide maximum illumination of the road without causing other drivers to be dazzled.

41 One essential fact to be remembered when riding at any time is that the rider should always be in a position to stop his machine well within the distance he sees to be clear. Even in ideal conditions, with the windshield, visor or goggles clean, and correctly aligned headlamp, the riders' view at night is restricted and he should adjust his speed accordingly. It should be noted that tinted goggles and visors will impair vision at night and in conditions of poor visibility.

42 A great deal of useful information can be obtained from the front and rear lights of other vehicles. A vehicle ahead approaching a bend from either direction could indicate the severity of the bend by the sweep of the headlights. When following a vehicle its brake lights will provide an early warning of the need to reduce speed. These are only two examples but there are many other occasions when intelligent use of information supplied can be of assistance to the rider.

43 When leaving brightly lit areas speed should be kept down to allow sufficient time for the eyes to become accustomed to the change of environment.

Dazzle
44 When a rider meets opposing vehicles showing headlights he should refrain from looking directly into them and cast his gaze slightly to the nearside. Should the approaching vehicle have headlights on main beam a quick flash of the headlamp may serve as a reminder to the other driver. Care should be exercised when doing this to avoid dazzling the other driver and on no account should retaliatory measures be taken. A rider should always be prepared to slow down or stop if he is dazzled, bearing in mind that the eyes need time to re-adjust.

45 When following another vehicle the headlamp should be kept in the dipped position and a generous distance between the vehicles allowed so as to prevent the leading driver being dazzled by lights showing in his mirrors. The machine should be moved out early prior to overtaking and the headlamp kept in the dipped position (except for a quick flash in lieu of a horn warning) until alongside the vehicle being overtaken. In the same way a rider being overtaken should dip his headlight when the following vehicle draws alongside and keep it in that position until it can be raised without dazzling the other driver.

Fatigue
46 Riding at night calls for great concentration and this, combined with dazzle and ever changing conditions of visibility, quickly results in tiredness. Once a rider realises that his riding skills are deteriorating he should reduce speed, and, if necessary, stop until he has regained his faculties fully. A walk or a hot drink may be all that is needed but any change from riding will improve the rider's capabilities.

CHAPTER 5

POSITIONING

Introduction
The system of motor cycle control requires at feature one, that the machine be in the correct position at the approach to any hazard. A good rider is always in the correct position on the road, not only when an obvious hazard is present, but at all times. Correct positioning enables the rider to obtain the best possible view of the road ahead and increases his margin of safety in relation to the actual and potential dangers around him. Positioning is clearly related to many other aspects of riding, such as cornering and road observation.

Safety Position
2 This may be defined as the safest position for a motor cycle to occupy on a road in relation to the actual or potential dangers existing at that moment.

3 These dangers usually arise from situations on the nearside, such as parked vehicles, pedestrians stepping off the footpath and concealed junctions. Where such dangers exist it would be safer to take a line nearer the crown of the road to obtain a better view and more space in which to take avoiding action should it become necessary. If, because of traffic conditions this plan cannot be adopted, speed must be reduced to ensure that no danger will be caused. Similar safety measures should be taken when riding on the offside of the road in one-way systems.

4 When passing a row of stationary vehicles there is always the possibility of pedestrians stepping out from in between them or a door opening. The view in between these vehicles is always very limited but it can be improved, if traffic conditions permit, by giving them a wide berth so providing a safety margin as well as a better view. Similarly the view into a road on the nearside can be improved.

5 Figures 9a and b show two motor cycles approaching such a hazard. The rider who is travelling quite close to the nearside cannot see very far into the road on the left and therefore fails to observe the vehicle approaching. The other rider positioning well towards the crown of the road has improved his line of vision and can see the approaching vehicle. The good rider will

always try to ensure not only that he is able to see as much of the road ahead as possible but that other road users can also see him. However it is important for a motor cyclist to be aware of road surface conditions and take full account of them when positioning. It would be foolish to position away from one danger only to fall off on a patch of mud.

Following Position

6 When keeping a position in traffic flows where there is no intention to overtake, a safe distance must be maintained behind the vehicle ahead. As a guide for normal riding conditions, one yard, per mile, per hour should be allowed but in built-up areas at speeds below 30 m.p.h. such distances are impracticable if traffic flows are to be maintained. In such circumstances, a minimum distance of one foot, per mile, per hour should be allowed. (To enable the rider to accurately assess distances, he should bear in mind that the average family car is about fifteen feet in length.) These distances are the minimum required as stopping distances increase greatly with wet and slippery roads, poor brakes, worn tyres and tired riders.

7 By keeping at the proper distance from the vehicle in front the rider will gain the following advantages.

(a) He will be able to maintain a good view, which can be increased along the nearside or offside by very slight deviation, so that he is always aware of what is happening in the immediate vicinity.

(b) He can stop the motor cycle safely in the event of the preceding driver braking firmly without warning.

(c) He can extend his braking distance so that a following driver is given more time in which to react.

(d) He can move up into an overtaking position when it is safe to do so.

8 In figure 10a the motor cyclist is following too closely to the vehicle in front. He cannot see any of the hazards in the shaded area. In figure 10b he is maintaining a good safety position and all these hazards can then be seen. He can improve his view by moving slightly to his nearside or offside.

Positioning for Turning and Stopping

9 When approaching a junction with the intention of making a left or right turn the rider should position according to the

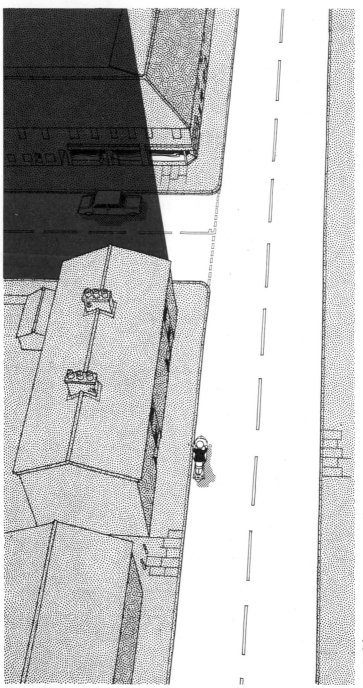

Figure 9a

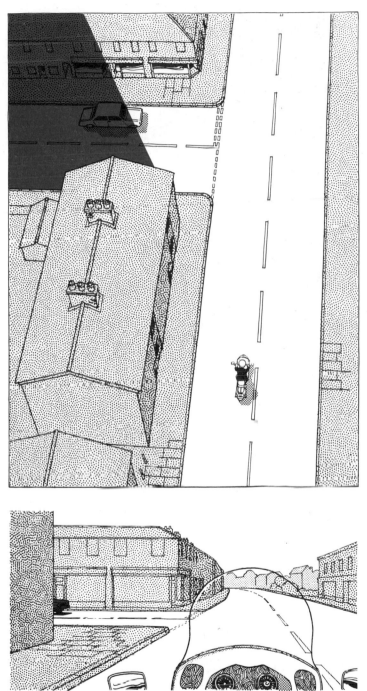

Figure 9b

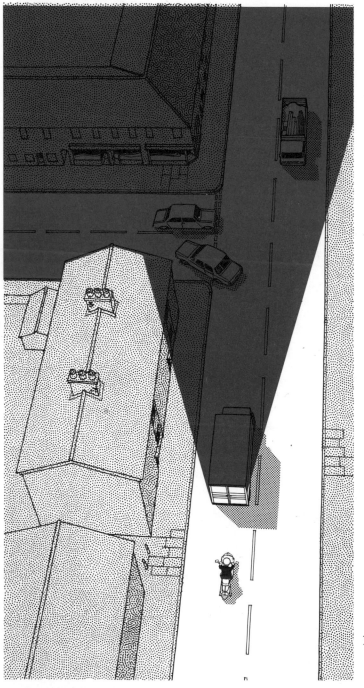

Figure 10a

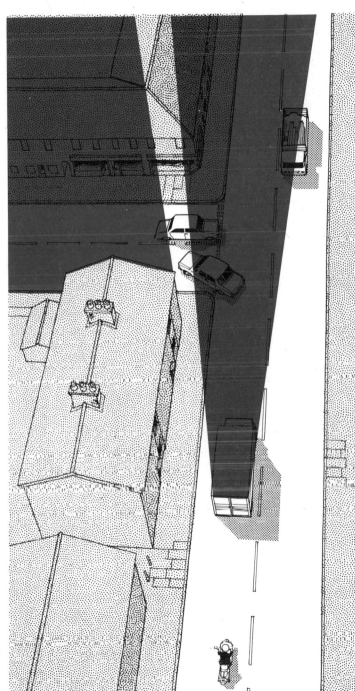

Figure 10b

turn, that is to the nearside of the road for a left turn and towards the centre line for a right turn. However, due consideration must be given to traffic light filter arrows, carriageway markings, other traffic and obstructions. Should traffic or road conditions make it necessary, positioning must always be adjusted in the interests of safety. For example, the rider intending to turn right must always be prepared to move away from the centre line when approaching traffic encroaches on his side of the road. Similarly when turning left the acute angle of the corner or the presence of pedestrians may require the approach to be further out than normal.

10 When turning right at crossroads, where opposing traffic is carrying out similar manoeuvres the vehicles should pass offside to offside. However, if the road lay-out makes this difficult or carriageway markings indicate otherwise the vehicles may have to pass nearside to nearside. This will be less safe if the riders' view of approaching vehicles is restricted as he turns.

11 When because of traffic conditions or obstruction of any kind it is necessary for the rider to bring his machine to a standstill he must give thought to his next manoeuvre and position his motor cycle so that he can carry out that manoeuvre with the minimum inconvenience to himself or other road users.

12 As a final word on the subject, parking the motor cycle must also be considered. It must never be left where it can cause inconvenience or danger to others.

CHAPTER 6

CORNERING

1 Cornering is a term used to describe the riding of a motor cycle around a corner or bend. It is an important feature of riding and a thorough understanding of the theory is essential if a safe technique is to be mastered. The manner of approaching and negotiating the various bends and corners encountered in day to day motor cycling will vary according to the conditions prevailing at each, but the following general principles must be complied with at all times to ensure maximum safety.

Principles
2 (a) Correct positioning of the machine on the approach side.

(b) Right choice of speed.

(c) Correct gear for the speed.

(d) The machine to maintain a constant speed when negotiating the curve.

Safety Factors
3 By application of these principles, the following safety factors will be apparent as the machine is about to leave the bend or corner;

(a) It will be on the correct side of the road.

(b) It will be able to remain there.

(c) It will be capable of being stopped in the distance the rider can see to be clear.

Machine Roadworthiness
4 The condition of the steering, suspension, tyres and tyre pressure and the loading of the motor cycle will affect the behaviour of the machine when negotiating a corner or bend. The riders' responsibility is to ensure that the machine and tyres are in good condition, tyre pressures are kept at those recommended by the manufacturer and any load carried is distributed evenly in fixed containers.

5 The road holding qualities of motor cycles vary considerably and an understanding of the characteristics of the machine being ridden, together with a sound knowledge of the

principles involved, will assist the rider to negotiate a corner or bend with minimum loss of stability.

Cornering Forces

6 A machine is most stable when travelling on a straight and level course at constant speed. When it is ridden around a curve certain forces are set up which affect its road holding capabilities and unless the tyres retain sufficient grip on the road the rider will be unable to maintain his selected course. The forces acting through the centre of gravity of a motor cycle are represented in figure 11 by arrows lettered 'M' 'C' 'R'.

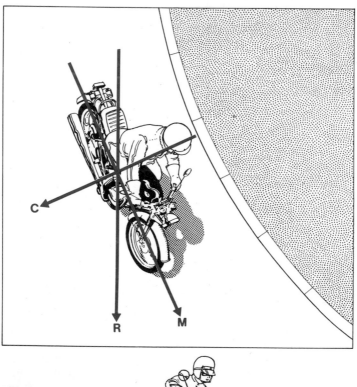

Figure 11

7 Arrow 'M' represents the momentum of the machine which is proportional to its weight and speed. The rider controls the momentum by selecting the correct speed. When the machine is banked over to enter a curve force 'C' is created. This is an outward pull known as 'centrifugal force'. In the figure, which illustrates a curve to the left, a combination of forces 'M' and 'C' produce a 'Resultant' force 'R', which tends to take the machine towards the offside of the road. Whilst considering the behaviour of the machine when cornering, it should be stressed that braking at this time is undesirable and may be hazardous.

Technique

8 It is only when travelling very slowly indeed when centrifugal force is practically nil that the front wheel of a motor cycle is actually turned into a corner. In these circumstances it is possible to ride the machine sitting almost upright. Most people, from their experience in riding a pedal cycle, know that, in order to take a corner at speed, it is necessary to bank the cycle towards the left on a left hand corner and towards the right on a right hand corner. Without considering why this is done it is apparent that if a rider attempts to ride round either corner at the same speed in an upright position he will be forced outwards towards the right of the road on a left hand bend and towards the left on a right hand bend — in all probability being thrown from his machine. By banking the cycle over as the corner is taken the rider is counteracting centrifugal force. This will have the effect of increasing the pressure on the wheels and thus the grip between the tyres and the road. This will be true up to a certain degree of banking so long as there is still a possibility of grip between the tyres and the road. How ever once this angle has been exceeded and grip has ceased centrifugal force will pull the wheels from under the machine and over it will go. In the same way, if the speed is low it is necessary to sit more upright otherwise the balance will be upset and the rider will fall towards the direction in which he is inclined.

9 It has been mentioned that the front wheel is not actually turned into a corner or bend except at low speeds. Banking the machine over to the left or nearside will automatically make it necessary for the rider to circle to the left. If he banked the machine and tried to continue riding in a straight line he would topple over. In just the same way banking to the right or offside makes it necessary to circle to the right in order to maintain balance. It will therefore be seen that when negotiating bends or corners at any but very low speeds all that is necessary to travel the curved course and at the same time overcome the tendency to be thrown outwards, is to bank the machine over without any movement of the handlebars, so that balance is maintained all the way round the bend. When the bend begins to straighten out the machine is gradually eased back into the upright position. Normally machine and body should be banked over together, but at higher speeds many riders will find that they have better control by banking the machine over while remaining in a more upright position themselves.

Road Camber or Cross Fall

10 The camber or cross fall of the road will also have a bearing on the effect of centrifugal force. A normal camber dropping from the crown of the road to kerb will be favourable when negotiating a left hand bend. It would be unfavourable on a right hand bend as the motor cycle will tend to slide down the slope more easily. Where the whole width of the road is super elevated with banking the cross fall will be favourable in either direction, thus reducing the effect of centrifugal force.

The System of Motor Cycle Control for Bends

11 To apply the principles correctly a rider must be able to appreciate early the different types of bend. This can only be achieved by good advanced observation. It is stressed that merely to observe the road disappearing into a curve will be insufficient. It is essential to look across the bend for gaps in hedges or between buildings to look at the road verges, hedgerows and lamp standards, etc., not only to make an assessment of its severity but to seek early warning of additional hazards.

12 Occasions will arise when it is impossible to obtain any information of this nature, leaving only one way to make the assessment. At the approach to most bends the offside and nearside verges appear to meet. This is the limit point of observation. (See figure 12.) The rate at which the limit point moves as the motor cycle approaches indicates the severity of the bend, i.e. if on the approach, the limit point appears to remain fixed and the view round the bend does not improve then, without doubt, the bend is sharp. On the other hand if the limit point begins to move away a more gradual bend is to be dealt with.

Positioning on the Approach (Feature 1)

13 When approaching any bend the rider must position his motor cycle to maintain the best view and from the information thus obtained his position may be adjusted to provide the maxi-

Figure 12

mum margin of safety and maintain the maximum stability as he negotiates the bend within the limits of his own half of the road. If bad road surfaces make it necessary positioning must always be subordinate to the interests of safety.

Right Hand Bends

14 The correct position on the approach should be close to the nearside. Figures 13a and b show how the view around such a bend is affected by positioning. However, before selecting a course consideration must be given to:

(a) Nearside dangers which would require a greater margin of safety, e.g. a blind junction or exit.

(b) Poor condition of road surface on the nearside or adverse camber.

Left Hand Bends

15 On the approach to a left hand bend advantage can often be gained by positioning the machine close to the centre line with the object of obtaining an earlier view. Figures 14a and b show how the view around such a bend is affected by positioning. However, before selecting a course near the centre line consideration must be given to the following:

(a) Offside dangers which require a greater margin of safety, e.g. approaching traffic.

(b) If such positioning may be misleading to other traffic.

(c) Where no advantage can be gained due to the low speeds involved or the open nature of the bend.

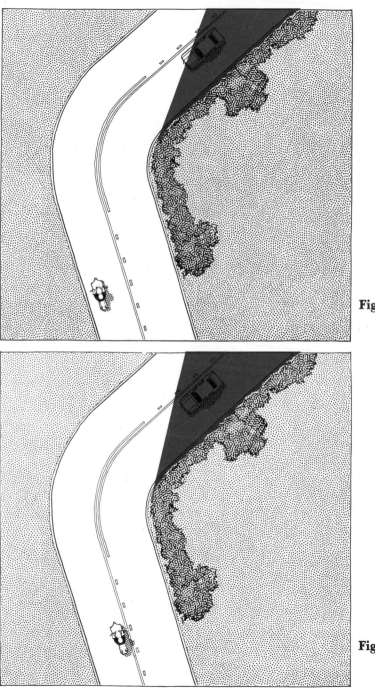

Figure 13a

Figure 13b

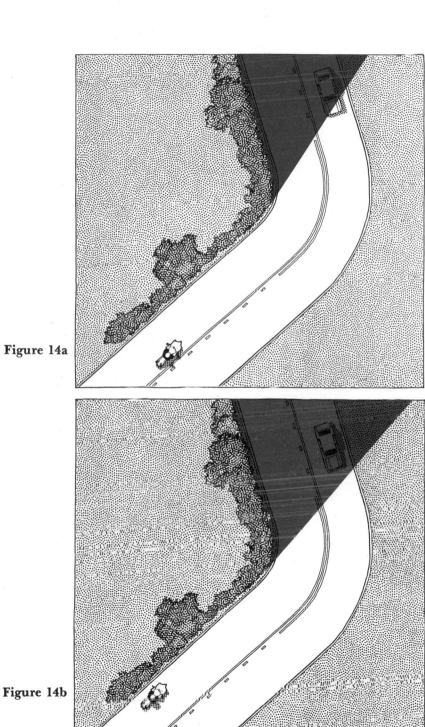

Figure 14a

Figure 14b

Right Choice of Speed (Feature 2)

16 Rear observation must be taken before reducing speed for the bend. Although an arm signal at the approach to a bend is very rarely required it should be considered. Where it is necessary to use the brakes to ensure the correct speed of approach the rules of braking must be complied with. The right choice of speed will be governed by:

(a) The view into the bend.

(b) The severity of the bend and the width of the road available.

(c) The state of the road surface.

(d) The actual or possible presence of other road users.

(e) The riders' ability and the road holding qualities of his machine.

Correct Gear for the Speed (Feature 3)

17 A safe speed having been achieved the gear must be selected to provide the increased power necessary to ride around the bend at a constant speed with the engine just pulling the machine and in which it will respond readily to the use of the throttle.

Rear Observation and Signals (Feature 4)

18 A rearwards check will ensure that the rider is fully aware of the situation behind before entering the hazard although a signal is not normally required at this point.

Horn (Feature 5)

19 Audible warning of approach is not normally required except perhaps when approaching acute blind bends, particularly on narrow roads where safety margins are restricted.

Rear Observation (Life Saver) (Feature 6)

20 A life saver check is not required at the approach to a bend.

Acceleration (Feature 7)

21 Ideally the gear selected enables the machine to negotiate the bend at a constant speed with the engine just pulling but there will be circumstances where this will not apply and where deceleration, and even braking may be necessary, for example:

(a) When descending a hill.

(b) Where other traffic makes it unsafe.

The point at which acceleration can be applied will be governed by the contours of the road, the state of the road surface and the rate at which a clear view ahead opens up. This point will vary, from just past the apex, to where the road straightens.

NEGOTIATING THE CURVE

Right Hand Bends
22 Previous paragraphs have dealt with the course selected to

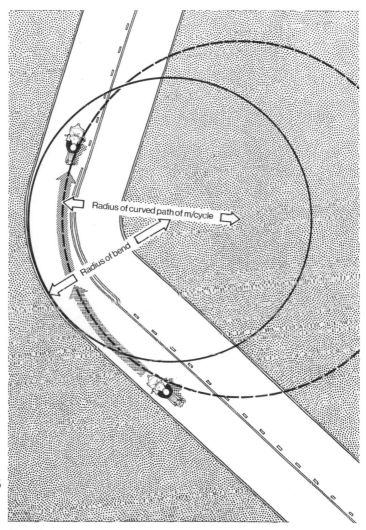

Figure 15

obtain the best view when approaching bends. For a right hand bend this was close to the nearside of the road. The rider maintains this course until he can obtain a clear view of the road as it straightens. Having gained this view he selects a gradually curving path towards the centre of the road, provided it is clear. He should then ease the machine back towards the nearside of the road. It will be seen from figure 15 that the radius of the curved path around the bend exceeds the radius of the bend itself and by following the shallower curve the effect of centrifugal force is reduced thereby improving stability.

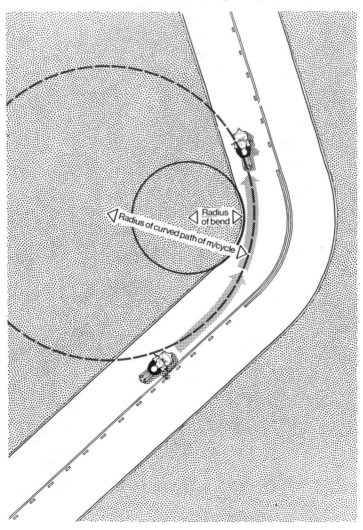

Figure 16

Left Hand Bends

23 When negotiating a left hand bend the position towards the centre line is maintained until the view ahead opens up. The machine is then ridden through a gradual curved path towards the nearside of the road thereby achieving the same advantages as when negotiating a right hand bend (see figure 16).

Provided that the rider has positioned correctly and in good time, adjusted speed, chosen the correct gear ratio for the particular type of bend or corner and maintained good observation whilst approaching and negotiating it, there should be no difficulty in achieving the required safety factors. The rider must always position his vehicle according to dangers which become apparent to him. IN NO CIRCUMSTANCES MUST ANY OTHER ROAD USER BE ENDANGERED OR INCONVENIENCED.

CHAPTER 7

OVERTAKING

1 A rider during his journey may pass many stationary and moving vehicles but those travelling in the same direction as himself he is said to 'overtake'. The System of Motor Cycle Control to be applied to the overtaking manoeuvre is the same as that described for fixed hazards. It is more complex however because during the process a number of subsidiary hazards may arise which must be dealt with as the primary hazard itself moves along the road.

2 A stationary vehicle on the nearside of the road requires some thought but presents little difficulty. Frequently the rider need do nothing beyond take rear observation before pulling out to pass the obstruction. On other occasions, when approaching traffic makes it unsafe to pass straight away, he must vary his speed and gear; perhaps stop altogether. The horn may need to be sounded if the vehicle is occupied or there are signs of activity in or around it. If the obstruction is not a stationary vehicle but a slowly moving one it is often possible to regard it as stationary for practical overtaking purposes (e.g. a heavy lorry going uphill). As its speed increases planning becomes more difficult and judgment more critical.

3 When a rider realises that he is catching up with another vehicle he makes up his mind either to adjust his speed and follow it while it makes reasonable progress, or overtake at the first opportunity. The decision to overtake is taken soon after the vehicle in front is sighted although the opportunity to do so may not arise for several miles, if at all in some circumstances.

Road observation
4 Thoughtless overtaking is highly dangerous and observation, planning and attention to detail are of the utmost importance. The overtaking rider must have a full and constant view of the road ahead and an understanding of the possible pitfalls. The course selected at this early stage is the position on the road from which the best view ahead can be gained subject, obviously, to no danger or inconvenience being caused to approaching or following traffic and without encroaching over hazard line markings, etc. Things to be looked for are obstructions on the nearside which may cause the vehicle in front to

move out (possibly without warning), bends, hill crests, junctions etc. where overtaking is dangerous and, on roads carrying two-way traffic, approaching vehicles. Painted lines on roads give warning of approach to hazards and arrows give an indication of a double line system ahead.

Planning

5 At most places where overtaking is forbidden by the Highway Code the dangers are self-evident but many riders overtake quite happily at junctions in the belief that traffic emerging from a side road will allow them right of way. Figures 17–21 illustrate some common accident situations when overtaking at junctions.

6 When overtaking the rider should aim to comply with the following:

(a) Never cause the overtaken or an approaching vehicle to alter course or speed;

(b) Avoid making a third line of vehicles abreast, either travelling in the same or opposite directions;

(c) Always be able to move back into the nearside in plenty of time.

7 In the absence of approaching vehicles or other hazard the rider need only take rear observation, move out onto a course to pass the vehicle with plenty of room and move back to the nearside of the road after overtaking without cutting in. No change in speed or gear may be necessary from when the vehicle is first seen to when it is overtaken and the only other feature of the System to be actually applied may be the horn. However, more often than not an approaching vehicle, bend, hill crest etc. will be seen and a decision taken as to whether the overtake can be completed safely before arrival at the hazard or not. On the approach to a bend or hill crest this means making allowances for a fast vehicle coming into view from the opposite direction. Judgments must be made in which experience plays a great part and must include an assessment of the speed of vehicles concerned and distances involved, such as:

(a) Speed of vehicles to be overtaken.

(b) Speed and performance of own machine.

(c) Speed of approaching vehicle(s) in view.

(d) Possible high speed of approaching vehicles as yet unseen.

Figure 17
Driver 'B' moves out looking to h right as 'A' approaches on wrong sid of road.

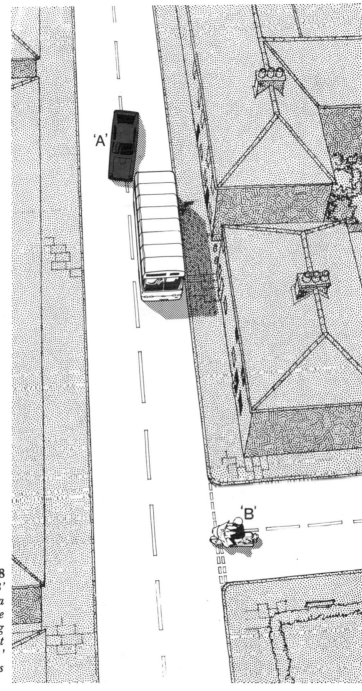

Figure 18
Rider 'B'
sees only a
slow vehicle
approaching
nd moves out
as 'A'
overtakes

(e) Distance available to overtake and re-gain nearside relative to (a) to (d) above.

The safe maxim is 'IF IN DOUBT HOLD BACK'.

8 Road observation will vary from immediate foreground through middle distance to far distance and back again with frequent glances in the mirror. It is not enough just to see everything, the correct interpretation has to be made. The driver of a small, crowded saloon car in front may have his attention diverted between what is going on inside and outside the car. A delivery van driver approaching a parade of shops may see his delivery point at the last moment and swerve suddenly across the road. Similarly, the long distance driver may turn off into a cafe. A high vehicle or caravan could be affected by a side wind. The type of vehicle to be overtaken must therefore be taken into account, as must the performance of the motor cycle being ridden. For instance if riding a low powered motor cycle and wishing to overtake a heavily laden lorry, the best time may be when going uphill as the speed of the lorry falls.

9 Different types of road present different problems, which will vary according to whether they are in the country or in town, but the condition of the road surface is

Figure 19
Rider 'A' is beckoned o- by driver 'B' into path o[overtaking car.

Figure 20
*Vehicle 'B'
turns without
warning into
an entrance
as 'A' goes to
overtake.*

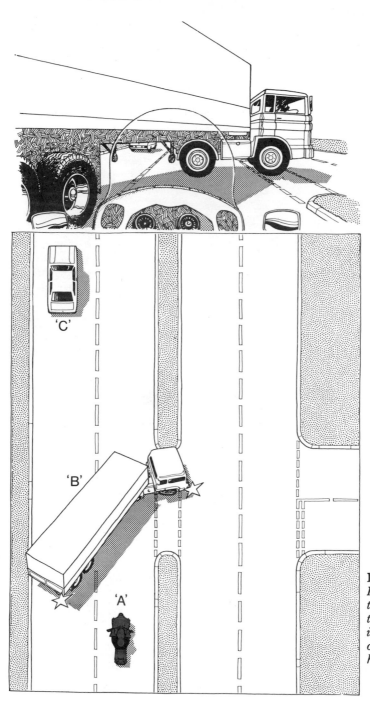

Figure 21
*Rider 'A' fai
to appreciat
that driver '
is not
overtaking v
hicle 'C'.*

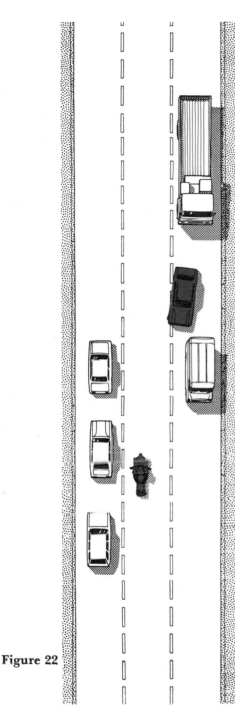

Figure 22

always a factor to be taken into account. There may be ruts which can throw a vehicle off line or surface water which will result in a curtain of spray at a critical moment. The effects of side winds must be taken into account when passing or overtaking high sided vehicles.

10 The most dangerous road carrying two way traffic is the one marked with three lanes, the overtaking lane each way being the centre lane. Overtaking must not be attempted on such a road if there is the possibility of an approaching vehicle moving out into the centre lane or when the overtaking vehicle would make a third line of moving vehicles, 'the meat in the sandwich'. (See figure 22.)

11 When judging speed and distance to overtake with a vehicle approaching the 'lurker' must be looked for, i.e. the small fast car or motor cycle which closes right up behind a lorry and then swoops out into full view (see figure 23).

12 It cannot be assumed that the driver of a light vehicle or car following a heavy lorry is content to remain where he is. He has probably been following too closely and with no idea of what lies ahead. He could pull out to take a look just as a following rider accelerates to overtake both vehicles.

Figure 23

13 The temptation to follow another vehicle through an apparently safe gap must be resisted. The leading vehicle could slip into a place of safety in the nearside leaving the trusting follower stranded in the middle lane faced by oncoming traffic (see figure 24).

14 Each rider must make up his own mind when it is safe to overtake and, when passing several slower moving vehicles, always have a gap in the nearside lane into which he can pull if necessary without cutting in. (See figure 25.)

15 Dual carriageways eliminate the need to assess the speed and distance of approaching vehicles but otherwise still demand the same degree of care. Speeds are mainly higher and drivers tend to move out from the nearside to change lane with less regard for following traffic. The wider the road the more this occurs, especially on motorways. As the overtaking position is approached vehicles in the nearside, and the middle lane if appropriate, must be watched. If one of them is closing up on a vehicle in front it is certainly going to pull out, possibly with no signal but probably with a trafficator switched on at the same time as the steering wheel is turned. A good guide is to note the distance between the wheels of a vehicle and the lane markings. If the gap narrows it could be moving out. Overtaking at a time which would cause three vehicles to be abreast of each other should be avoided, if possible.

16 It is often possible by the use of acceleration sense to vary the speed a little on the approach so as to arrive at the overtaking position just at the right time. Where this is not possible speed will be reduced to that of the leading vehicle in order to follow in line at a safe distance.

17 From his 'Safety Position' (see Chapter 5) the rider having decided that an overtaking opportunity is developing may move up into an overtaking position. The view ahead must be maintained for movement of other traffic, parked vehicles, other obstructions and any physical feature of the road which may make it unsafe to overtake.

Right Hand Bend
18 Where the leading vehicle is approaching a bend to the right where the view is restricted the following rider should select a course well to the nearside, moving up on the vehicle in front just before it reaches the apex of the bend so that he gains the earliest possible view along its offside (see figure 26). If conditions are favourable a straight course should be adopted to

Figure 24

overtake with adequate near-side clearance. If conditions are not favourable for over-taking the rider must drop back and resume his safety position.

Left Hand Bend

19 Where the leading vehicle is approaching a blind bend to the left the following rider must not attempt to overtake until the road is straight. He should maintain a position where he can see along the nearside of the leading vehicle as it passes through the bend. If this view is favourable he may move out to look along the offside as the road straightens and start to overtake when conditions are suitable (see figure 27), bearing in mind that when changing from a nearside to an offside view, areas of the road ahead will be obscured. Great care must be taken when carrying out this manoeuvre.

System of Motor Cycle Control

20 When conditions are suitable to overtake the course is selected to pass with plenty of room bearing in mind that the higher the speed the greater the margin required for safety. A rear observation will be necessary to see if a signal need be given before moving out (System of Motor Cycle Control, feature 1). If already on course to pass, no signal will be given. At feature 2 a

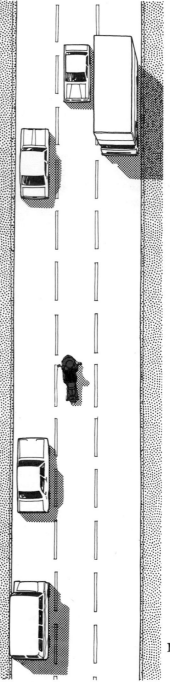

Figure 25

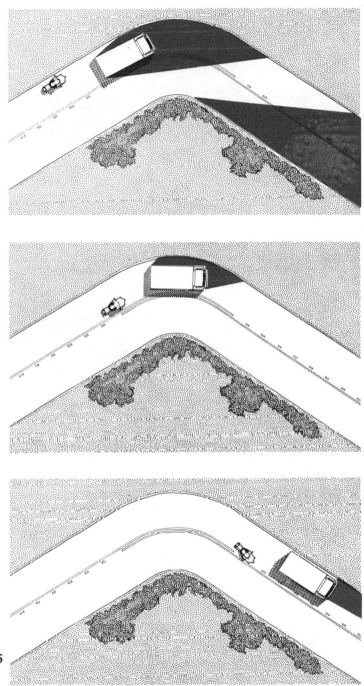

Figure 26

Figure 27

further rear observation will be taken but a signal would not be needed nor would speed be adjusted. At feature 3 the gear will be considered to give the best acceleration within the speed ranges to be used in the manoeuvre; although the alert rider should already be in the right gear. A final rear observation at feature 4 is worthwhile but no signal would normally be of any use at this point. The horn (feature 5) is frequently a vital safety factor, particularly if more than one vehicle is to be passed at once or there is a possibility that the driver in front may not be aware of the presence of the overtaking vehicle. The 'Lifesaver' (feature 6) is unecessary. In fact, to be looking back whilst commencing an overtake could be positively dangerous.

21 A motor cycle travelling alongside another vehicle is in a zone of danger in which it does not do to dwell too long. Overtaking should therefore be completed as quickly as possible (feature 7) but before he reaches the rear of the vehicle in front the rider still has an opportunity to change his mind and drop back.

22 Overtaking calls for judgment and expertise which can be acquired only by experience and practice. As skill and the judgment of speed and distance are developed mistakes can be made. It is important for the rider to realise this and for him to make sure that his decisions err on the side of safety. Patience must be exercised at all times and a margin of safety left for error.

CHAPTER 8

SKIDDING

Skidding is defined as:

1 The involuntary movement of the motor cycle due to the grip of the tyres on the road becoming less than a force or forces acting on the machine. In other words a motor cycle skids when one or more of the tyres lose normal grip on the road.

2 A rider who has experienced a skid will remember that he was changing either speed or direction of the motor cycle immediately prior to the skid developing. It will therefore be realised that skids are usually caused by accelerating, braking or changing direction. These manoeuvres being carried out so suddenly or forcibly that forces are created which are more powerful than the grip of the tyres on the road. It therefore follows that the more slippery the road surface the less powerful these forces need to be to break the grip of the tyres.

3 Figure 28 shows a motor cycle and the forces which may operate are indicated by arrows:

(a) Is created by acceleration.

(b) Is created by deceleration (usually by braking).

(c) Sideways forces created by the rider when banking the machine over to negotiate a turn to the left or right.

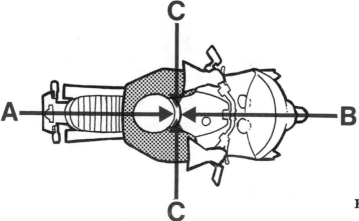

Figure 28

These forces act on a motor cycle when the rider operates the controls, but they should never be permitted to become so powerful as to overcome the grip of the tyres on the road. Two of these forces are combined when the motor cycle follows a curved path when under the influence of braking or acceleration.

4 The following are the causes of skidding, either singly or in combination:

(a) Excessive speed for the existing circumstances—this is a basic cause.

(b) Banking the machine too far over when turning and cornering.

(c) Harsh acceleration.

(d) Excessive or sudden braking.

Recognition and Correction of Skids
5 It is essential that each type of skid is recognised as early as possible if corrective measures are to be taken.

Rear Wheel Skid
This occurs when the rear wheel loses its grip on the road and the machine may swing in either direction. It can be caused by (a), (b), (c) or (d) of paragraph 4 and if unchecked can cause the machine to turn broadside completely out of control. Eliminate the cause by easing off the throttle or the brake and bring the machine into an upright position concentrating on steering. When stability has been regained the throttle or brake can be re-applied but to a lesser degree than before.

Front Wheel Skid
6 This occurs when the front wheel loses its grip on the road and may be caused by (a), (b) or (d) of paragraph 4. Although by eliminating the cause it may be possible to regain control there is so little time to recognise, react and correct this type of skid that every effort must be made to avoid it. In the event of the motor cycle being banked over and the front wheel suddenly regaining its grip the machine will be unbalanced and on a course other than the one desired. Effective control may be restored by adopting the upright position.

To Minimise the Risk of Skidding
7 Every rider should aim to ride and control his motor cycle in such a way that it does not skid. Good road observation, with

accurate interpretation of what is seen, is necessary in order that all road conditions may be accurately evaluated and speed adjusted accordingly. Some obvious hazards such as snow and ice are recognised by most riders as dangerous surfaces. Few appreciate that a shower of rain after a long dry period can produce conditions where skidding may occur because the accumulation of rubber, dust and oil, together with water, creates a very slippery surface.

8 Almost every type of surface gives a reasonable grip to the tyres at very low speeds but as speed increases this grip value falls rapidly on some surfaces and recognition of potentially dangerous areas is essential. Some examples are given in Chapter 4 paragraphs 17–24. To realise the surface is bad only when the machine is running over it is too late.

9 The importance of an adequate depth of tread and correct pressures in the tyres must again be stressed as neglect of these factors will increase the risk on slippery roads.

10 When riding on very slippery roads smooth control is essential. Any braking, accelerating, steering or gear changing must be carried out so that tyre adhesion is not broken. When moving off or travelling at low speeds the selection of a higher gear than normal may be advantageous to reduce the possibility of wheel spin.

General

11 If a skid is allowed to develop fully a rider will rarely find that he has enough space to correct it. Concentration and good observation are essential if skids are to be avoided and quick reactions are necessary when a skid does occur.

It is important to again stress that on very slippery roads the best control of the speed on a vehicle is through the throttle with a suitable gear engaged.

Reduction of the speed on a slippery surface is best done by the selection of a lower gear but it is essential that the gear change is made as smoothly as possible with accurate matching of engine revolutions to the road speed before the clutch is finally engaged.

12 Loose surface riding instruction is given for three reasons:

   (a) to raise the standard of riding to give the highest degree of all round efficiency;

   (b) to give confidence in riding under any conditions; and

   (c) to equip the rider to meet any emergency which might arise.

CHAPTER 9

General

1 Improvements in vehicle design and road engineering over the years have led to motor cycles capable of achieving and maintaining a high speed with safety especially on roads designed for this purpose. Without a similar raising of riding standards any advantages offered by such improvements will be lost. Not every rider is capable or desirous of using these improvements to maintain high speeds and, of course, not every road is suitable. Speed is frequently looked upon as something dangerous in itself, but it is dangerous only if used in the wrong place or at the wrong time. Speed then is a relative thing.

2 What to a novice may be a dangerous speed is not necessarily so to a more experienced rider. The choice of speed must be related to the rider's ability, the type, condition and limitations of the machine and the prevailing road and traffic conditions, bearing in mind that the safe speed for any given section of road may vary from minute to minute as circumstances alter.

3 Statutory speed restrictions in respect of areas and classes of vehicles assist in reducing instances of dangerous high speed but legislation by itself is not sufficient for on many occasions the maximum permitted speed will be too fast for safety. Remember the onus is always on the rider to select a speed appropriate to the conditions, for example, although 30 m.p.h. may be permitted through a shopping area to ride at that speed at certain times of the day might be positively dangerous.

Speed—Its Affects on the Rider

4 How vision is affected by speed has been mentioned previously, but the importance of first class observation again needs to be stressed. Observation is seeing and assessing the road ahead to enable a safe riding plan to be made. This becomes more difficult as speeds increase. Travelling slowly a rider can afford to direct his attention to things in the immediate foreground. Although a rider should automatically focus his eyes and attention further ahead when driving faster, few fully appreciate the importance of making a special effort to do

this by varying the length and width of vision to take in the most distant features and not miss important lateral detail.

5 After travelling at fairly fast speeds upon the open roads, it will be noticed that when speed is brought down to 30 m.p.h. on entering a restricted area it seems as if the machine is crawling along. After a while the sensation of travelling slower than the limit disappears but it will always recur following an appreciable reduction in speed after driving fast for a prolonged period on the open road. In these circumstances it is always advisable to look at the speedometer before entering a restricted area, roundabout or other hazard. Be especially careful when leaving a motorway.

6 A frequent check on the speedometer is always valuable as speed is difficult to judge in some circumstances. When travelling along narrow and winding country lanes even moderate speeds appear to be high while the impression of travelling fast would not be apparent on an open road at that speed. At night, or in conditions of reduced visibility, speed is deceptive and may be much higher than the rider realises. The rider of a quality motor cycle should not be misled into thinking that the speed of the vehicle is lower than it is in reality due to the lack of noise and vibration which may be present in less expensive models.

7 Travelling at high speed requires total concentration and mental application. If these speeds are maintained over considerable distances fatigue will result. The rider should also be aware of the danger of being called upon to ride at a high speed after prolonged periods of riding at normal speeds. He may already be tired or not mentally attuned to the task and must make allowances or errors of judgment will result.

Use of Speed

8 Efficiency in riding at speed is not easily acquired. Every rider has his own speed limit, the highest speed at which he is perfectly safe and comfortable in any given situation. He should never attempt to go beyond that limit for if he does he may be late to react to an emergency. When circumstances make it necessary to ride at high speed it is of vital importance to remember and put into practice all that is set out in this manual. At 30 m.p.h. a minor error can be rectified. At 70 m.p.h. the same error can have disastrous consequences.

9 Speed must be governed at all times by the amount of road that can be seen to be clear, therefore, high speeds are safe only

when a clear view of the road ahead is possible for a considerable distance. A motor cyclist must always be able to stop within the range of his vision by day or by night. In this respect local knowledge can be a dangerous thing as it is tempting to ride faster than is safe on a familiar road. Many people drive too fast where hazards exist because they do not recognise actual or potential danger and in the belief that they will be able to stop whatever happens. A rider should not only know his stopping distances but be able to relate them to the road on which he is travelling. On a single track road due allowance must be made at all times for the possibility that another vehicle may appear around the next bend. Because of the combined speeds the distance available for braking may be halved.

As may be seen from the table in Chapter 2 if speed is doubled then the braking distance is quadrupled, i.e. speed 30 m.p.h. — braking distance 45 feet. Speed 60 m.p.h. — braking distance 180 feet.

10 When riding fast the need to overtake other vehicles will occur more frequently. Overtaking is a potentially dangerous manoeuvre and must be carried out as quickly as possible. It will always call for accurate judgment of the distances involved and the speed of any approaching vehicle. The speed of the vehicle to be overtaken must also be considered but generally this is easier to determine because it can be judged by the speed at which it is being overhauled.

11 Adverse weather conditions no matter what the cause, be it rain, snow, fog or wind, may demand a drastic reduction in speed to keep within the bounds of safety as excessive speed in these conditions is a basic cause of skidding. If the road surface is wet then the allowance for braking distance should be at least doubled whilst on icy stretches it could be in excess of four times that required in normal circumstances.

12 High speed on stretches of road affected by heavy rain or surface water can be hazardous and lead to 'Aqua Planing'. This is a condition in which the front tyre loses contact with the road surface due to the formation of a wedge of water which forces itself between tyre and road. This results in loss of directional control. If a rider suspects that his machine is or is about to aqua plane the application of brakes even momentarily may aggravate the condition by breaking the last small contact between tyre and road. Control will not be regained until speed has been reduced by deceleration.

Under normal motoring conditions the factors necessary for true aqua planing are heavy rain, a smooth tyre, a smooth or badly drained road and a speed in excess of 50 m.p.h. Extremes of any of these conditions permit the others to be less stringent.

13 A rider should always take time to familiarise himself with the controls and characteristics of a motor cycle to which he is unaccustomed before attempting to ride fast.

To Sum Up

14 (a) Do not ride at high speeds unless you are competent and it is safe to do so.

(b) Do not relax for an instant. Use all your skill and concentration.

(c) Always ride so that you can pull up in the range of your vision whether by day or by night.

(d) If you double your speed you quadruple your braking distance.

(e) Put into practice all principles covered in other chapters.

(f) Guard against the effects of fatigue.

(g) No emergency is so urgent as to justify an accident. It is far better to arrive late than not at all.

CHAPTER 10

GENERAL ADVICE AND TEN COMMANDMENTS

Condition of Motor Cycle

1 Every rider is responsible for ensuring that his machine is in a roadworthy condition and the following items should be checked.

(a) Visual examination of the whole machine. Check around for damage and defects and underneath for traces of oil or fluid leakages.

(b) Check that the gear is in neutral.

(c) Tools carried and securely stowed.

(d) Wheels, ensure they are secure, no loose or broken spokes or rim damage.

(e) Tyres, check pressure, tread depth and for damage. (Tyre pressure readings will not be accurate unless the tyre is cold.)

(f) Brakes. Check adjustment and correct operation of systems.

(g) Cables. Free operation, not dry, frayed or trapped.

(h) Horns.

(i) Lights and electrical equipment.

(j) Oil and fluid levels as necessary.

(k) Petrol, ensure sufficient for journey.

(l) Check tension of drive chains, if fitted, in accordance with manufacturers' recommendations.

(m) Take machine off stand and check that stand is properly stowed.

Pre-Riding Check

2 Before moving off the rider should familiarise himself with the position and operation of the controls and instruments. The following routine should be carried out.

(a) Remove machine from the stand.

(b) Check that the gear is in neutral.

(c) Check position of controls and auxiliaries.

(d) Turn on the petrol.

(e) Raise level of petrol in the carburettor (where applicable).

(f) Free clutch plates, where necessary, by operating the kick start lever with the clutch lever depressed.

(g) Switch on ignition, note operation of warning lights. (Choke to be used as required in accordance with manufacturers' directions.)

(h) Set throttle.

(i) Operate starter. When the engine is cold use kick start to conserve battery.

(k) Check gauges and ensure that warning lights go off.

As soon as possible after moving off the rider should carry out a running brake test (see Chapter 2 para. 44). At intervals throughout the journey all instruments and warning lights should be checked and the necessary action taken if a fault is indicated.

Conspicuity
3 In other than good visibility road users may find it difficult to see motor cyclists because rider and machine offer a small silhouette and can easily be lost against the general background. To reduce this risk to a minimum the rider is urged to wear light coloured or reflective type clothing.

Stopping and Leaving the Machine
4 When intending to leave the machine the rider should bring it to rest in the most convenient and safe position, close to the kerb if on a road. It should not be parked close to the rear of a large vehicle as it may not be clearly visible in the other driver's mirrors when he is manoeuvring. The motor cycle should be placed on the main centre stand whenever possible but not on soft surfaces such as new tarmacadam or where there is a camber. If the machine is left on the side stand it should be in first gear so that it cannot roll off the stand. The side stand should not be used in strong winds or where the slip-stream of passing traffic could pull the machine over. The machine should be properly secured if it is to be left unattended with the petrol taps in the off position.

Riding through Water

5 To ride at speed into water may wrench the front wheel out of line and may cause the rider to lose control. Particular care is necessary at night when the difference between a wet road surface and flood water is difficult to detect. Flood water will collect quickly at the sides of a cambered road, where the road is undulating, where there is a dip under a bridge and in poorly drained low lying areas. On the approach to flooded areas reduce speed considerably and avoid riding through water if possible by making intelligent use of the unaffected parts of the road. If, however, this is not possible choose the shallowest section to ride through, bearing in mind that there may be hidden obstructions or subsidence. If the route is entirely submerged stop the motor cycle and assess the situation. The depth of water which can be successfully negotiated varies with the type of motor cycle, having regard to its ground clearance and the position of the electrical components. Having decided to ride on the following procedure should be adopted:

(a) Engage first gear and keep the engine running fast by slipping the clutch, in this way the water will be prevented from entering the exhaust pipe even when it is submerged.

(b) Maintain a slow and even speed to avoid making a bow wave.

(c) Immediately after passing through deep water ride slowly with the brakes lightly applied until they grip. Repeat this procedure until satisfied that the brakes are fully efficient.

Remember that river fords often have a deposit of extremely slippery vegetation upon the submerged road surface, and the rear wheel of the machine must be well clear of the water before any acceleration is applied.

Cleaning the Machine

6 Care should be taken when using pressure hoses to clean the machine. Water under pressure will not only enter brake drums and settle on disc pads but also force grease from some of the more exposed bearings on the machine, particularly steering and suspension parts, causing corrosion and inducing premature failure of the components.

TEN COMMANDMENTS OF MOTOR CYCLING

1 Perfect your roadcraft

Roadcraft includes every aspect of riding and can be acquired only by a systematic approach to hazards and constant application of the basic rules. Good roadcraft enables a rider to avoid awkward and possibly dangerous situations. It not only prevents accidents but makes riding less arduous.

—Use your skill to keep out of trouble.

2 Ride with deliberation and overtake as quickly as possible

Good riding demands continual planning and correct decisions which must be put into operation with deliberation. There is no place for the half hearted manoeuvre born of doubt or uncertainty. If it is not completely safe it should not be attempted at all.

Overtaking should always be completed in the minimum of time to leave the road clear for approaching or following vehicles.

—Deliberation eliminates uncertainty. When safe, go!

3 Develop motor cycle sense and know the capabilities of your machine

Motor cycle sense is the ability to get the best from the machine without jerks or vibration. Before a strange motor cycle is ridden fast the rider should accustom himself to its controls, acceleration and braking capabilities and handling characteristics. Never expect more from them than they are able to give. Motor cycles, like riders, have their limitations.

—Rider and machine must blend to ensure skilful riding.

4 Give proper signals, use the horn and headlights thoughtfully

Use the signals given in the Highway Code. An ambiguous signal is misleading and dangerous. Use of the horn is a form of signalling much neglected by some and overdone by others. It should be used as a person would use his voice, neither aggressively nor rudely. Flashing the lights is an efficient form of signalling at night and on fast roads.

—Give good signals in good time.

5 Concentrate all the time to avoid accidents

Concentration is the keystone of good riding. It is a primary duty but often a neglected one. Complete concentration will ensure that every detail is observed. It is often the smallest detail that gives the clue to what is about to happen. If it is missed an accident, or at least an unpleasant experience may result.

—Concentration assists observation.

6 Think before acting

The good rider makes progress so smoothly and with so little apparent fuss or effort that to the uninitiated he appears to respond to situations automatically. Nothing could be further from the truth. The fact is that by continuous concentration and thought he has raised his riding to a fine art.

Every hazard and riding operation presents problems which can only be solved by thinking. A thoughtful rider applies the appropriate features of the system, carries out every operation and manoeuvre in plenty of time and consequently is always in the right place at the right moment.

— *Think and avoid accidents.*

7 Exercise restraint and hold back when necessary

To hold back is to follow a vehicle at a safe distance until road and traffic conditions allow it to be overtaken. This will call for restraint especially when in a hurry. Overtaking, or any other manoeuvre must never be attempted unless it can be completed with 100 per cent safety. Accidents are caused because a situation has been wrongly assessed.

— *Whenever in doubt, wait.*

8 Corner with safety

Riding around a curve demands the application of the principles for cornering and a thorough knowledge of the forces acting on the motor cycle. The most common faults are entering too fast or accelerating before the exit is clearly seen.

- *Lose your speed or lose the machine.*

9 Use speed intelligently and ride fast only in the right places

High speeds are safe only when a clear view is available for a considerable distance and there is time to assess each hazard as it appears, but speed at all times must be related to the view. Safety with speed depends largely upon ability to recognize danger and to slow down in good time.

— *Any fool can ride fast enough to be dangerous.*

10 Know the Highway Code and put it into practice

The Highway Code sets out rules for safety on the road. A failure to observe them could establish liability in any legal proceedings. The rules must be known and complied with if a rider's own behaviour is to be beyond reproach and before he can presume to advise others. The Highway Code urges all to be courteous. A good rider goes further and acknowledges the courtesies extended to him.

— *Ride according to the Highway Code and you will ride safely.*

NOTES

Printed in England for Her Majesty's Stationery Office by
Ebenezer Baylis and Son Limited,
The Trinity Press, Worcester, and London.
Dd 596117 K48 3/79